DISEASES OF FREE-RANGE POULTRY

DISEASES OF FREE-RANGE POULTRY

including hens, ducks, geese,
turkeys, pheasants, guinea fowl,
quail and wild waterfowl

VICTORIA ROBERTS, BVSc MRCVS

Whittet Books

FOR JACK

First published 2000
Text © 2000 by Victoria Roberts
Illustrations © 2000 by Victoria Roberts
Whittet Books Ltd, Hill Farm, Stonham Rd, Cotton, Stowmarket,
Suffolk IP14 4RQ

British Library Cataloguing in Publication Data
A catalogue record of this book is available from the British Library

Photographs on the following pages are reproduced by kind permission
of Intervet UK: 56, 57, 69, 72, 73, 81, 88, 96. All other photographs are
by the author. Line drawings by the author.

ISBN 1 873580 53 3

Printed in Hong Kong by Wing King Tong

CONTENTS

FOREWORD

I have always been fascinated by poultry. This enthusiasm stems from my lifelong interest in birds and other wildlife. From an early age I recognised the debt that the human race owes the domestic fowl - as a source of meat, eggs and feathers, as part of many cultural traditions and as a key to numerous scientific discoveries. I was entranced by the story of the domestication of the Red Jungle Fowl and how its all so familiar descendant gradually spread throughout the continents to the extent that it now supplies 20% of the world's animal protein. That the ancestor of *Gallus domesticus* is still extant and yet so little studied added spice to the tale and reinforced my belief that the key to all animal care is an understanding of the species' behavioural needs and an interest in its natural history.

As a veterinary student in the 60s I took comfort from the fact that, although we were taught nothing on our university course about the other 9,000-odd types of bird, our tuition *did* cover the domestic fowl, the domestic duck and a handful of other avian species. As a result I gained a sound grounding in poultry management and diseases which, coupled with my own knowledge of keeping and treating other kinds of bird (ranging from avadavats to zebra finches), helped to prepare me for a varied career in veterinary medicine.

In Britain and other Western countries keeping free-range poultry has gone through a cycle from where (pre Second World War) it was the norm, followed by several decades of decline - as birds were housed intensively - to a new phase whereby more and more people are interested in maintaining free range birds or voluntarily opt for their eggs or meat. What is forgotten, of course, is that in much of the world, keeping poultry 'free range' is standard practice - not because owners have strong feelings about the welfare of their birds and the benefits of providing 'natural' conditions, but because they can afford nothing else. I refer, of course, to the countless millions of domestic chickens, ducks, geese and guinea fowl that roam villages in Africa, Asia and South America. In Tanzania, East Africa, for example, where I first worked as a volunteer veterinary officer after qualifying in 1966, these local poultry were my patients on a daily basis. I was expected to be able to catch them (not easy!), to handle them and to diagnose ailments in individual birds. Treatment was sometimes medical, such as giving an injection, often surgical, such as repairing a torn crop. The situation is little different in many places, even 35 years later. In Tanzania, for instance, it is estimated that there are over 25 million village chickens - more fowls than people - and that country, as in so many parts of the world, these birds play a vital role in providing food for the human population. What makes local poultry so remarkable is that they are able to convert a mixture of local vegetation, invertebrates and refuse into meat and eggs. These same birds play an important role in rural communities - not only on account of their acceptability as a food source to most religious groups, but also because in many African and Asian countries it is the women who tend the poultry, thus enhancing the role and status of these members of society.

So I welcome Victoria Roberts' new volume not only because it will assist those who keep free-range poultry (of all species) in the UK and other relatively wealthy countries. Her book will also be of great practical value to people who work in poorer locations overseas and, in so doing, it will help to raise the profile and well-being of that often overlooked gift to the human race - the local chicken.

Keeping poultry is fun - and never more so than when these birds are able to express normal behaviour in a stimulating environment. Being 'free-range' does not, however, mean that such birds are protected from disease: they are merely exposed to different dangers and different stressors from their housed counterparts. Recognition of disease - and, indeed, of health - in such birds requires powers of observation as well as veterinary knowledge and Victoria Roberts is uniquely qualified to teach these. She leads a remarkably full life, much of which revolves around the countryside and the keeping of animals. She shares her home with a fascinating array of livestock and yet still finds time to continue her veterinary studies - and to write books! I have the greatest admiration for Victoria and am delighted that she is soon (through her own tenacity and hard work) to join the veterinary profession. In so doing she will bring with her years of experience and that sound, commonsense, attitude to animals and their welfare that is so needed in our society. As the populace becomes more urbanised, both geographically and psychologically, understanding of our responsibilities to the Animal Kingdom become muddled. Victoria's approach, expressed so well in her writings, will help to ensure that more rational, but no less humane, attitudes will prevail.

This is an excellent book that will do much for free-range poultry and for those who tend and care for them.

Professor John E Cooper
DTVM, FRCPath, FIBiol, FRCVS
Durrell Institute of Conservation and Ecology (DICE), University of Kent, UK
Consultant Veterinary Pathologist, Jersey Zoo
February 2000

INTRODUCTION

Birds and man have been inseparable for centuries, each having learnt to trade off the other for food and exploit any available opportunity in a long history of association. Chickens derive from the Red Jungle Fowl (*Gallus gallus*, a small pheasant of Asia) and have been documented for at least 4,000 years as providing fresh meat, eggs, feathers and some truly horrible medicines. Domestic geese are descended from the greylag (*Anser anser*) and as well as meat, eggs and down, feathers also provided excellent fletching for arrow flights when the bow was a common weapon.

Domestic ducks are all descended from the lascivious ubiquitous mallard (*Anas platyrhynchos*) and rather surprisingly hold the laying record of all poultry: 364 eggs in 365 days. The muscovy duck (*Cairina moschata*) has its own niche in meat production as it is a larger, separate species (the perching ducks: beware the sharp claws) with more meat, used mostly in France. Humans have been using poultry for medicinal purposes (recipes are in Pliny's writings in 4BC and *Aldrovandi on Chickens*, 1598, for example) with the cure seeming worse than the affliction, for a great deal longer than we have had either the means or desire to treat the birds: a bird either survived or it did not in days past, being individually not particularly valuable compared to a larger food animal, and having a much greater capacity to reproduce in a short generation time.

In the desire to produce cheap food for a burgeoning human population, poultry was intensified, the main advances being in the early 1950s. This meant that flocks were brought indoors to avoid predators, parasites and soil-borne diseases. Hardy pure breeds were originally used to create the ubiquitous broiler and hybrid battery hen, but the subsequent development did tend to concentrate on production to the detriment of hardiness. Unfortunately, the intensification created ideal conditions for other opportunistic bacteria and viruses to multiply and spread in the confined areas. Many modern poultry diseases can be traced to this intensification, but that is somewhat balanced by the tremendous research then done on diseases and production, to the benefit not only of poultry but also human medicine. There are umpteen good textbooks on industrial poultry diseases containing a plethora of long words (which, should you be able to understand them or remember them, would make you a champion at the childhood game of 'Hangman') but they are not particularly helpful for free-range birds.

In the year 2000 I expect to graduate as a vet. I have kept poultry both commercially and privately for the past 30 years, served on the Council of the Poultry Club of Great Britain and been the Secretary of the Dorking Club for the past 10, and had to learn the hard way about free-range diseases.

This book is therefore a distillation of experience (with thanks to some poultry scientists and vets) and is aimed at the person who wishes to keep their free-range hens or waterfowl healthy. I will try to give guidance on good management, common diseases and problems; also to explain why certain problems are more likely to occur due to a bird's very different body systems from a mammal's. The principle of being able to drive a car without knowing how it works is all right for inanimate objects but not good enough for animals under our care. Incidentally, 'poultry' covers other domesticated bird species too, such as turkeys, guinea fowl, quail and pheasants. Some 'long words' are used for the sake of precision - anything not immediately understood or explained will be found in the Glossary. A quick reference table of symptoms which I first developed for the Poultry Club's set of Basic Leaflets should prove useful. The poultry keeper will spend much time just observing the birds and this is invaluable and necessary. Positive signs of health need to be known in order to realise that there is something wrong, which sounds obvious, but most texts only cover problems. The great secret with all bird keeping is to be able to recognise signs of ill health as a deviation from normal in the early stages.

Because they are a prey species, birds have an ability to disguise symptoms of disease until it is really too late. This is usually the stage when a vet gets to see them, so if a bird can be presented to a vet at an earlier stage of a disease there is a much greater chance of a treatment being successful, thus improving welfare at the same time. We all still have a great deal to learn.

Victoria Roberts, 1999

1 POSITIVE SIGNS
OF HEALTH

As with most animals, the positive signs of health must be studied in order to know when something is amiss. In chickens, the signs of health are dry nostrils, a red comb (some breeds have naturally dark ones), bright eyes (colour varies with breed), shiny feathers (all present), good weight and musculature for age, clean vent feathers with no smell, smooth shanks, straight toes, and the bird alert and active. Some of these can be established by observation and others by behaviour and handling (see below). Other poultry species follow similar parameters.

BEHAVIOUR

Many common conditions or diseases of poultry can be avoided if something is understood about their behaviour. Poultry are creatures of great habit - life is safer that way - so any change in routine can upset them. This can range from a sudden snowfall, when they will not venture outside as the ground has changed colour, to a sudden change from meal to pellets, one of which does not look like food.

This is where people call them stupid, but this nervousness is of course part of the survival mechanism. The key word here is 'sudden'. They will cope with most changes if they are gradual, so put food and water in the hut until the snow is accepted and, if changing food, do so by mixing the two types together for a few days. Birds do not have much sense of taste but they are sensitive to texture. They use shadows to spot potential food items on the ground and anything falling or moving is immediately investigated. All birds have colour vision and hens are particularly attracted to red, hence the red bases to chick drinkers. Unfortunately this also means that any fresh blood is also attractive which can lead to cannibalism, no matter how large the area of range, but once the blood has dried the danger is usually past. Hens make very bad gardeners - they seem to be convinced that everything you have planted is upside down. What they don't scratch up, they dust bathe in. Ducks prefer to be able to sieve everything in sight, so like to add water to soil, creating a muddy mess in no time. They are their own worst enemies in a small area in winter and do better on flags or fine gravel which can be hosed down if grass is not available. Geese prefer short grass but cannot live and produce on this alone, especially as grass has very little food value from August to April, but they are also fond of debarking trees, so protect any vulnerable trunks.

The word 'henpecked' is so much part of our language that most would use it without thought to its origin, but the pecking order is a vital component in maintaining the stability of the flock in hens and to a lesser extent in waterfowl. With or without a cockerel, hens have a strict hierarchy and territory which only changes if a bird is removed or is sick. How then do you return a recovered bird to a small flock? With great care and supervision, as their memory is very short and the whole structure has to be reshuffled. The recovered bird must be fully fit in order to reclaim her place. If hens fight, the cockerel will usually break it up. Should you wish to add, say, three or four new laying hens to an established flock, the least traumatic way to do it is to turn their liking for routine against them and put old and new into a fresh henhouse so no-one has established a territory. Young, unconfident laying hens cannot be expected to start or continue to lay if being bullied by the rest of the established and confident flock: youngsters can quite easily be killed by the matriarchs. Old English Game are best left to the experts as even chicks out of the same clutch will kill each other.

Turkeys tend to have only one idea in their heads at a time, so if they have decided to pick on another bird it is usually fatal. Although waterfowl are less aggressive they can still dominate food or water and thus deprive a newcomer, so add more food and water bowls to counteract this. Geese pair up in the winter and will often reject a new goose if added in the spring, so if you wish to mix and match, do so in August when the pair bond is at its weakest. Wild waterfowl tend to choose their nesting sites in the winter, so get boxes and shelters organised early. Unlike waterfowl, hens can be immensely stupid in rain. The older ones will quickly decide if it is only a shower or a lasting downpour and run for home, but young birds are liable to stand around in the wet looking miserable. They will get hypothermia (low body temperature) quite quickly, especially those with thin skulls and crests such as Polands. It is a fast downward spiral as they then do not have the energy to find shelter or food and the wind chill factor increases dramatically when birds are wet. A Silkie will even brood her chicks in the rain as her maternal instinct is stronger than her survival instinct. This is why people wanting broodies prefer a Silkie cross (Sussex is good) so that the maternal instinct is still strong but with an extra dose of common sense.

Anything overhead or flying is a potential predator - the comical way waterfowl tip one eye to the sky will often alert you to a sparrowhawk or buzzard and then there is a general buzz of alarm to warn the others. Geese and other waterfowl make good guards as they sleep with just one half of their brain at a time, leaving one eye open, and their reactions are very fast. Waterfowl night vision is excellent, unlike hens, so they prefer to sleep outdoors, but unless an area is foxproof, this is asking for trouble. They are quite easily trained to go into a hut as they herd well. Hens do not see well in the dark so they feel safe in a dark enclosed space at night, putting themselves to bed before twilight, but they do not herd well, even in daylight; two long bamboo canes can work wonders in getting them all to go in the desired direction. Turkeys herd well, but they prefer to stay up later than hens.

Quail and pheasants are usually kept in aviaries as they fly so well. They can be kept free range if wing feathers are clipped (see page 43) but pheasants moult their wing feathers at different times, unlike waterfowl which drop the lot at once, so you can be caught out by a suddenly escaped bird, which has moulted enough primaries to get off the ground. Wildfowl are either clipped once a year or pinioned at birth (see page 43).

Waterfowl have the instinct to imprint on the first moving thing they see when they hatch. This is vital if they are living wild as they have to follow their mother immediately. It is useful to tame (as opposed to imprint) waterfowl by regular handling, particularly just after they are hatched and this works well with artificially incubated domestic and wild waterfowl. As long as they have others to be with the rest of the time it does not upset later breeding behaviour. Remember that anything above their heads is a threat from day one, so approach low and quietly but talking all the time.

HANDLING

Handling on a regular basis is very important as it is usually the only way to tell if a bird has lost weight or not - even when emaciated their feathers disguise this fact, so handling will give a vital early clue to any problems. Not only loss of weight but excess weight can be assessed by feeling the pin bones either side of the vent: they are sharp if the bird has little fat and well padded if obese. The distance between them will tell you if the hen is laying (see page 79). If you can weigh birds as well, then so much the better. Habituating birds to being handled should start as young as possible, but if adult birds are acquired they can soon be tamed down by frequent handling.

With hens it is best to begin at night so they are quiet and sleepy; move quietly and talk all the time. Slide your outstretched hand, palm up and fingers spread, under the hen. Her breast should rest on your outstretched palm, her legs clutched between your first/second and third/fourth fingers. Your other hand is placed over her back to balance her as you lift her off the perch. Take the weight on your forearm and hold her close to your body, her head pointing towards your armpit, leaving your other hand free to inspect the bird. This principle of holding applies to all species and all sizes of poultry - the bird is balanced and comfortable and the mucky end is away from you. When lifting a bird off the floor, use two hands to restrain it around the wings and then transfer one hand under it with outstretched palm, as above. Some bantams get very tame, such as Pekins, and will happily ride around on a shoulder. Never catch a bird by one leg as the hip will dislocate with horrifying ease. A fishing landing net is very useful for catching a bird outdoors - about a 24" (60cm) diameter and 6' (2m) handle will cope with anything from bantams to geese and reduces stress, both for you and the bird (stress and normal egg production do not go together). In order to maximise the life of the net, remember to keep the handle and net in a straight line, so once the net is over the bird, drop the handle onto the floor, effectively containing the bird while you extricate it. To get a bird out of a cage or showpen, slide one hand over its back, turn it to face you, get both hands around both wings, lift, pull through the cage door, and then transfer to one palm. To get a bird out of a cardboard box safely, push your hands blindly in the top thin slot so it cannot fly out and grasp the body around both wings as before. Wild waterfowl and pheasants are better allowed to get out of a carrying box on its side in their own time if they are in their final pen.

The only chicken that is liable to peck you is a broody on her nest and that is only a warning. Some cockerels take against certain people: counteract this by picking up the offending bird and cuddling it the first time it attacks - if you retaliate you are merely reinforcing the behaviour. I have not found a cure once the bird thinks it can get away with it, apart from the final one. What is amusing in a tiny bantam is of course downright dangerous in a large cockerel, particularly with children. Geese can be serious about nipping as they bite and then twist, which can be excruciating, but if you have its head under your arm, as above, it can do little damage. Beware your shins if attempting to look at a goose on her nest - the leading edge of the wing is used as a most efficient cudgel. Either leave well alone, or be brave and grasp the goose firmly around the neck at arm's length once off the nest - she will sit down and you can then pick her up as before, her head always pointing behind you. Warn any children to steer clear. Ducks rarely bite, but do beware of muscovy claws: not only are they sharp, but the ducks are extremely strong for their size.

It is permissible to pick a duck up with fingers around the base of both spread wings in one hand, middle finger pointing down the duck's back, for a very short transfer distance - useful in small, wriggling wildfowl whose legs are vulnerable to damage. Domestic ducks may be picked up by the base of the neck, again, for a short transfer.

When applying dusting powder against lice and mites, hold the bird in one hand as before and lay it on its back, using your forearm to hold it down. Your free hand is then used to powder under the wings and tail and rub in the powder, using a glove. Thin gardening gloves are useful to avoid scratches when handling many poultry.

SEXING

As chickens have very similar external reproductive parts, sexing is done by appearance with the adult cocks having larger combs, flowing plumage and (usually) spurs. Some breeds of chicken can be sexed when day-old such as Welsummer (females have better defined markings) or Marans (the male has a larger white spot on its head) but neither of these methods is better than 80% accurate. Vent sexing is really not an option for small-scale breeders of chickens - either the variation between breeds is too great or the numbers do not warrant the cost of using professional sexers. Some sexers are currently advertising to sex hatches of over 200 and specify pure breeds. However, at around 8-10 weeks old, there appears on the backs of the cockerels pointed, shiny feathers which the hens never have (see page 18).

Older birds in some breeds can be sexed by their plumage colour, such as black breast in male Silver Grey Dorkings. Female chicks grow their tail and wing feathers before the males do during the first three weeks. Trusting the comb development to be 100% correct is not feasible as its development is affected by many different factors. Silkies, with their fluffy, unstructured feathers, are impossible to sex until at least 16 weeks old with any certainty: a fact which some unscrupulous breeders use to full advantage on newcomers. Wait until they crow! Waterfowl are much easier as they have a protrusible phallus which can be seen from day-old. The best and easiest time to search for this is between one and

How to hold a duck for vent sexing.

four weeks. Place the duckling or gosling on its back, its head towards you. The vent is carefully but firmly opened between both thumbs with a sideways motion, pushing from the back with the fingers, and the penis exposed: this looks like the point of a biro. If the vent is like a rose with petals then that is the female (see overleaf). Between one month and adulthood the males and females look very similar, even to an expert, and this is the time when people can get caught out, especially with geese and wildfowl. Adult geese and ducks have a spiral phallus with a tight vent, the female vent continuing to look like a rose but looser than the male. Female domestic ducks quack (as opposed to rasp) at about 8 weeks and the adult males grow 'sex curls'. If these are missing, check the voice. Muscovies have no voice unless really stressed. They can be vent sexed, but the males quickly grow to be half as large again as the females with caruncles (red fleshy lumps) on their face.

Do not assume a pair of waterfowl is male and female just because they go around together. Single sex 'pairs' are quite common with dominant and submissive behaviours.

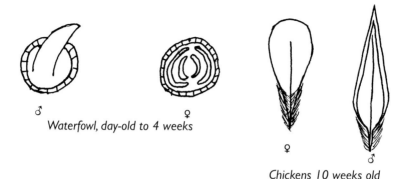

♂   ♀
Waterfowl, day-old to 4 weeks

♀   ♂
Chickens 10 weeks old

Turkey males tend to have larger shanks and feet than females and the females retain feathers on their heads. Even so, it may take until 14 weeks to decide for sure, except for the bronze where the hens retain white lacing on the breast. The adult stag turkey is significantly larger than the hen, displays frequently with its extendible snood, upright tail and grows a tassel of coarse hair from its chest. Guinea fowl are best left until mature at 16 weeks when the females will develop a double syllable call. Do not rely on shape or size of wattles to distinguish the sexes.

Quail are mature at 6 weeks, the male having a plain breast and the female a spotted breast, except for the white ones. Breeding males of any colour have a pointed tail and often have foam around the vent, the females laying at 6 weeks old. Pheasants may not attain their full colour until one or two years old, depending on species, but the Game Pheasant colours up from about 12 weeks.

IDENTIFICATION

It is useful to be able to identify individual birds from a point of view of keeping records. Some wildfowl have by law to be close ringed (a printed, permanent ring put on the leg when very young) in order to be sold or transferred. The Poultry Club runs a Ringing Scheme with a different colour printed ring for each year and there are various designs of plastic removable rings: coloured flat ones for chickens and spiral ones for

The principle of injection into the breast muscle of a bird: parallel to the ground if the bird is on its back and to one side of the breastbone. The Welsummer bantam had been snivelling, so 0.5ml of Tylan was administered. The yellow colour of the drug can be seen in the syringe barrel.

waterfowl as they don't pull these off. Some breeders use numbered wing tags placed in the leading edge of the wing. It is not easy keeping track of a clutch of chicks as they are generally too small to ring: either use a permanent marker pen on them or clip some down from their heads as this is the final area to feather up, by which time they can be leg ringed.

DRUG ADMINISTRATION

There are various ways of administering medicines to poultry, some involving handling. Probably the easiest is in the water, but it is not always the most effective, as all other sources of water must be removed and the solution must be replaced regularly, some drugs breaking down quicker than others; a sick bird may not want to drink. Some drugs can be added to feed, either by the owner (wormer) or already mixed by the manufacturer such as coccidiostats or wormers. Poultry can be drenched or crop tubed if they will not drink, or oral drops administered. Some drugs come in a tablet form and these are relatively easy to put down the throat of a bird. Louse powders and preparations are usually applied topically either in powder form, spray or drops. Probably the most efficient route of administration for antibiotics is intramuscular injection, usually in the breast muscle, which is safer than the leg; but flying birds are better injected in the leg. Depending on the drug, there may be some irritation at the site. Subcutaneous is not effective as the blood supply is limited; intravenous is difficult. It is imperative that drug withdrawal times are adhered to and the correct dose and correct course of drug given - there is already much resistance to certain drugs with incorrect or over use. Records are mandatory for some medicines and it is a good idea to get into the habit of recording details in any case to improve management.

VACCINATION

There are several schools of thought on vaccination of free-range birds. Ideally, they should be fit enough to acquire natural immunity. Wild birds carry all sorts of nasty diseases from other places, however, so a problem may arise. If it does, then vaccination may be the best way forward. There are risks involved with some live vaccines mutating, the specific strain of virus not being included in the vaccine, or the virus itself mutating rendering the vaccine useless. Concurrent disease or stress can also render vaccines ineffective. Marek's disease (page 95) affects certain breeds such as Silkies and Sebrights more than others and some breeders regularly use this vaccine. Other breeders consider that vaccines merely mask the disease and weaken the strain of bird. Current advice is that if there is not a problem, don't vaccinate; if there is a problem, use the right vaccine correctly. Vaccines are being researched and developed all the time, so contact your vet for the latest developments.

HYGIENE AND DISINFECTANTS

Clean water and clean water containers are probably the single most important aspect of hygiene. A murky bacterial soup of water is not conducive to healthy poultry. Keeping food dry and fresh is also important, with as little mud as possible anywhere. Poultry have evolved to live with a certain amount of their own muck and have always done well on deep litter systems as long as it remains dry and friable, their immune systems being continually gently boosted. High ammonia levels are toxic and these are worst on wet litter. Keep areas around water containers dry as coccidia flourish in the damp. Some breeders are obsessive about cleaning pens and cages every day: it simply is not necessary and may even be detrimental. What is necessary is looking at the muck and checking that it is normal - this is where a droppings board is useful. Use your nose and eyes. Anyone who has kept poultry will know the phenomenal amount of dust they produce. It is well worth vacuuming hen huts or sheds occasionally - the amount of cobwebs covered in dust will alert you that it is time again. Do wear a mask as you do it as dust is a haven for pathogens (bacteria, viruses and fungi) and just the right size to bypass our own not very efficient filter systems and get right down into our lungs. 'Farmer's lung' and allergic asthma are not worth acquiring. The most effective and least toxic disinfectants to both you and your poultry are Virkon and Antec Longlife 250S. Both have been developed specifically for poultry and their diseases. Virkon is used for cleaning chick equipment and incubators and Antec Longlife

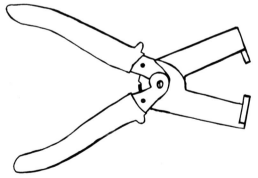

Semark pliers: a commercially available humane killer useful for chickens and up to medium-sized ducks. They dislocate the neck and thus sever the internal carotid arteries. Easy and efficient to use.

for larger scale equipment cleaning as it is more economical. As always, protect yourself with rubber gloves, and remove any muck or dirt before using the disinfectant. Other disinfectants are either toxic or not proven to kill all the bacteria and viruses poultry are susceptible to and most of them do not work in high levels of manure. Sunlight (UV light) and wind drying are very efficient methods of removing pathogens, but the equipment must be cleaned first and dismantled. Unfortunately, steady sunlight cannot be relied on in the UK.

CULLING

The time will come when you will have to cull. The most humane way of killing poultry is to dislocate the neck, thus severing all blood vessels and nerves to the brain. Practise on a dead chicken until you are confident how much strength it takes for the size of bird without pulling the head off. Ducks and geese are easier if the head is laid, chin down, under a broom handle on the ground, your feet either side of its head and then pull upwards with its feet. Or use the Semark pliers, previous page. Whatever method you use, they will flap afterwards, so be prepared for movement.

DEATHS

If a bird is found dead there are two actions: send it for *post mortem* investigation, suitably wrapped, to a specialist, or burn the corpse. Disposal of avian corpses in the dustbin is not appreciated, and leaving corpses around to encourage the proliferation of blowflies is not responsible. Deep burying in areas not frequented by your poultry, maybe under fruit trees to encourage recycling of the nutrients, is a better bet. Never contemplate eating any poultry that has died, unless you have killed a healthy bird for that specific purpose (at least you know the bird has had a good life, what it has been fed on and how it has died - unlike all supermarket poultry).

VERMIN CONTROL

Foxes, rats and mice will be your major regular visitors. Secure fencing will prevent the fox doing damage, or enlist the help of a local gamekeeper if one gets in. Rats and mice can be controlled - never eradicated as they always come in from elsewhere - with the use of strategically placed secure poison stations around the property. It is worth investing in modern bait stations as they are easy to service and secure from pets and non-target species. In the spring you may find magpies stealing eggs from inside the henhouse. If a bead curtain over the pophole is not effective, magpies can be controlled with the use of a Larsen trap. Again, seek help from a local gamekeeper. In some parts of the country mink are a serious problem, but are easy to cage trap. See Further Reading, for appropriate publications and Chapter 2 for parasite control.

For Management and Nutrition, see Appendix V, page 133. If these are right, your birds are more likely to stay healthy.

2 EXTERNAL ANATOMY: SKIN AND FEATHERS

Skin

Avian skin is more delicate and thinner than mammals' and is attached to muscles in relatively few places but firmly attached to the skeleton extensively on the foot and carpus (the end of the wing). Subcutaneous fat is known as 'bloom' on table birds ready for slaughter and the thick layer of fat under the skin of aquatic birds helps to keep them warm. Feather follicles are arranged in tracts, the elevation controlled by muscles under the skin with some areas free of feathers which helps with thermoregulation, as they have no sweat glands.

When a hen is broody, a bare area of skin on her breast, the brood patch, is in contact with the eggs to maintain moisture and temperature. Four-week-old chicks develop a synovial bursa (breast blister) normally at the front end of the breast which only becomes a problem if it gets infected by being on damp litter. Adult Old English Game have few feathers on this area normally and the Transylvanian Naked Neck has half the number of feathers of other chickens in order to cope with a hot climate, but they look a little strange with just a cap and gown - all exposed skin being bright red.

Normal skin colour is either white (e.g. Sussex), yellow (e.g. Rhode Island Red) or black (e.g. Silkie) and turkey head skin can change colour from white through red to blue, depending on mood. Leg colour again depends on breed or colour of plumage and in breeding cockerels there is a red blush down the legs. Yellow leg colour can fade in laying hens as the pigment goes into the yolk. The comb and wattles are very well supplied with blood vessels and in a fit mature bird are bright red (except dark-faced breeds, e.g. Silkie, Sumatra). Earlobes are either white, red or

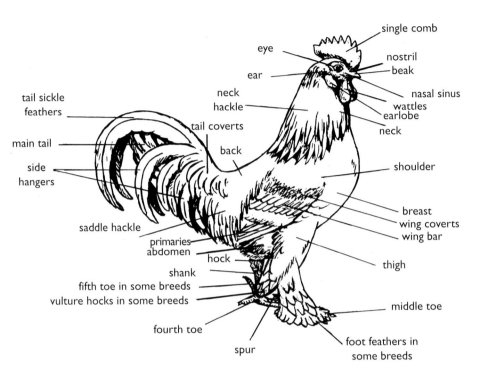

Some points of the male fowl

blue depending on breed and a white earlobe denotes the laying of a white shelled egg as they are genetically linked. Muscovies and turkeys have caruncles on their heads and necks which are enlarged, highly coloured areas of skin. The snood on a turkey is an erectile structure which in displaying males hangs down in front of its beak. It exists in females but does not change size. The beak is a structure made of hard keratin and continually grows throughout the life of chickens, turkeys and pheasants. Waterfowl have a softer, more pliable and very sensitive bill with which they sieve and find food. Claws are also of keratin and sometimes need trimming if there is no access to hard surfaces. Spurs can

The spur of the six year old Silver Grey Dorking is very sharp and will be filed down before he is put in the breeding pen so that he is less likely to damage the hens, although sharp claws can also break feathers and tear the flank of hens. The filing and smoothing has to be done every two to three years.

be found on both male and old female chickens, for example Sumatras and Dorkings.

A short round spur indicates the age of a male as less than six months. A longer, sharp spur (about 1", 2.5cm) denotes a bird of approximately one year old and spurs increase in length by about ½" (1cm) every year. Scales on legs are moulted once a year and should be smooth and shiny. Foot pads are like shock absorbers but can become infected in poultry or in waterfowl develop corns if surfaces are too hard or dry. Most waterfowl have straight webs of skin between their toes, but Nene geese normally have less web in a deep semicircle. There are glands in the ear canals which exude wax: the ear canals themselves are concealed by small tufty feathers.

The preen gland is a small, nipple-like protruberance just above the

26

The bronze turkey hen has sustained damage to her flank from the claws of the male but looked normal with just a few feathers missing from the outside. This wound is an old one and is healing, but continuous insult may lead to infection and death. The stag should not be allowed to get too heavy, but it is unusual for all his hens to be in the same state - this may have been his favourite. Buff Orpington hens can suffer in the same way as their feathers are soft and break easily, leading to exposure of the skin to the claws of the cock. Take the males out and only allow them limited access to the hens for fertilisation purposes (10 minutes every three days for example). People who exhibit their birds keep the cocks and hens mostly separate to avoid broken feathers.

tail. It exudes an oily substance which birds then preen over their feathers to help weatherproof them and keep them plus beak and leg scales in supple condition.

Problems/diseases

Discoloured comb:

white or pale: the bird may be anaemic, so check for mite infestation.

purple: the circulation is impaired which usually means a weak heart: cull or wait. Some birds manage well until stressed such as being handled or washed for a show.

black: this may be dried blood, so wash gently. If in winter it may be frostbite on the spikes of the comb and these can drop off. Cover other large combs at risk with Vaseline. If the blackness does not turn red when washed, suspect *Erysipelas* (page 29) in turkeys.

yellow: jaundice which may indicate avian TB (see page 98). No treatment.

white spots: fowl pox virus. Uncommon and may be vaccinated against. Pigeons are carriers, chickens, turkeys and quail affected. Spread by biting flies.

Chapped skin: In severe weather, keep birds indoors.

Breast blister: Should reduce by itself. If infected use tylosin.

Flank wounds: Mainly in turkeys or soft feathered hens such as Buff Orpington. Check for overgrown spurs or claws. Fit turkeys with a cloth 'saddle' or keep stag or cock separate. May need stitching and takes time to heal.

Ear infection: Normal wax exudate goes cheesy and yellow. Treat with dog ear drops.

Corns: Symptoms lameness, painful unusually raised area on base of foot; mainly in waterfowl, bathe feet and move to softer ground.

Bumblefoot/swelling of the pad of the foot: Infection caused by *Staphylococcus* bacteria. Check perches are not too high as bruising predisposes. If in early stages, try treating with homeopathic sulphur tablets or lincomycin. If chronic, surgery may be successful but is expensive. May need to cull if advanced. Difficult to cure.

Crossed beak: May be inherited or early trauma. Mild cases can be trimmed but advisable not to breed. Severe cases should be culled as soon as noticed.

Spur overgrowth: Bird will not be able to walk as spur hits other leg, or spur is growing back into leg; can be filed smooth if sharp point. There is a large artery in the spur so do not attempt removal without cautery.

Claw/beak overgrowth: They will not be symmetrical: trim with dog nail clippers to normal shape, being aware of the quick.

Vent pecking: Cannibalism usually occurs through overcrowding and/ or heat stress. Beak trimming is not the answer and is no longer recommended on welfare grounds. Remove any birds not already dead, use blue antibacterial spray to disguise red colour and reduce infection. Keep injured birds apart from the rest until completely healed and feathers have grown back.

Vent gleet/inflamed vent and with necrotic, yellow, moist covering: In hens this is thought to be a herpes virus passed on during mating, a venereal disease. Successful treatment is usually only temporary as the herpes virus lives in the nerves and reappears periodically. Theoretically, acyclovir should work, but the cost has precluded any field trials. The condition is rare, but it does not need to be spread around a flock, so affected birds are usually culled. Once smelt, the pungency of vent gleet is never forgotten. In waterfowl, vent gleet is caused by *Pseudomonas* infection and soiling of the vent due to not enough water to bathe or swim in. Being bacterial in origin it is treatable with a suitable antimicrobial if caught before the scarring stage which reduces the elasticity and diameter of the vent preventing egg laying and sometimes even defecation.

Erysipelas: Land with a history of sheep or pig production is liable to contain the *Erysipelas* bacteria; principally turkeys over 13 weeks are affected, pheasants and occasionally ducks, geese, chickens and quail. The organism can survive for years in the soil, so be aware also that problems may occur if a pond has been dug or topsoil imported. It enters birds through breaks in the skin, so fighting or biting insects can be a cause. Onset of disease is rapid with birds found dead in good condition. Poisoning is frequently suspected, such as ionophore toxicity (see page 47). Turkeys have dark, crusty skin lesions anywhere on the body, but particularly on the head. Ducks may have dark webs instead of orange. Heart disease is also caused by *Erysipelas*. Penicillin injection will bring an outbreak under control and there is a vaccine for turkeys. The danger of this disease is that it is zoonotic and can cause skin rash and cellulitis (swelling) in humans with possible heart disease for anyone handling infected carcases and sustaining an injury, such as a cut.

The cuckoo Dorking had a crossed beak since a chick and was grown on to see if she survived, but she is obviously coping well with it having grown to this size and laying. It is not always easy to spot a crossed beak in day-olds unless they have other deformities as well (such as one eye, bent legs or toes) and sometimes they can sustain damage to the beak in the first few weeks which makes it grow crooked. Birds with uneven growth on the beak, whether sideways or downwards, probably should not be bred from as this is inherited. Unscrupulous breeders will trim the beak to make it look normal.

A Partridge Wyandotte bantam with an overgrown top beak.

*A Barred Plymouth Rock bantam with feathers plucked out of his saddle area -
this is likely to have been done by one of his wives; however if this type of feather
loss is noted on a hen, it is probably due to the claws or spurs of the cockerel
when he has been mating her. Note the pointed cockerel feathers.*

Feathers

There are four types:

1) Contour feathers, which cover the body and include the wing feathers, the wing coverts, the tail feathers and the small feathers covering the ear canal. When these contour feathers emerge from the feather follicle they have a pulp cavity with an artery and vein; as the feather matures this is resorbed, creating a hollow tube: a broken growing feather will therefore bleed profusely, but mature feathers may be cut (as in wing clipping) with no damage. The strength and waterproofing of the feather is maintained by the barbs interlocking: as the bird passes the feather through its beak when preening, the barbs are relocked.

2) Very close to the follicle of each contour feather is a delicate filoplume (thread-like feather) which has many nerve endings and helps to keep the contour feathers in optimum positions. Plucking feathers on a live bird is therefore a painful process. The filoplumes remain after plucking a carcase and have to be removed by singeing.

3) Semiplumes are fluffy feathers with a shaft which act as thermal insulation and increase buoyancy in aquatic birds. Silkies have only semiplumes, leading Marco Polo in the 13th century to describe them as hens with wool on their backs.

4) Down feathers do not have a shaft and include those on newly hatched chicks; adult chickens have some in otherwise featherless areas and of course waterfowl have a complete layer under their contour feathers.

The colour of feathers is due to a combination of pigment and structure. Melanin pigments occur in granules in the skin and feathers and produce yellow, red-brown, brown and black. Carotenoids, derived from plants, produce yellow, red and orange in fat globules in the feathers. White colour in birds is caused by the reflection and refraction of all wavelengths of white light striking the feathers and iridescence by varying the structure of the feather.

Sexing of hens (not Silkies) can be achieved by observing the shape of the growing feathers on birds from about 8-10 weeks old. The rounded subadult feathers are replaced in the males by sharply pointed and shiny feathers between the shoulder blades and above the tail (see page 18). Adult plumage is attained by 18 weeks in most poultry but some pheasants can take two years for the males to colour up. For sex-linked plumage, see page 75.

Moulting is the shedding and annual replacement of feathers, usually after the breeding season. The new feather pushes out the old one from the base of the follicle and is vulnerable to damage while growing. Hens and turkeys moult swiftly once a year outside the breeding or laying season, but ducks moult twice a year, the drakes in the summer going into eclipse plumage which is similar to the female ducks' for camouflage as they are flightless for a few weeks at this time. Pheasants moult over a longer period, making wing clipping suddenly ineffectual as the primaries are sequentially replaced.

Sometimes the tail feathers of poultry can get stuck in the feather sheath. This can be gently removed with a thumbnail to prevent damage to the emerging feather. Old feathers can change colour due to weathering and wear, so the new set usually looks very clean and smart. If feathers appear which are a totally different colour from before, the bird may have nutritional deficiencies, or the ovaries may be damaged and a hen may produce a male set of plumage. This is fairly common in hens, pheasants and ducks and is known as intersex (see Sex Reversal, Appendix II). The birds usually neither lay eggs nor mate subsequently and it is generally irreversible. Sebrights and Campines are henny feathered and thus do not have the male feather characteristics: this is a feature of these breeds.

Hens, pheasants and turkeys like to dustbathe as it keeps their feathers in good condition and helps to remove any lice. Dry ashes, sand or dry soil is appreciated, so ensure a dry area in winter. Wing clipping is used to prevent birds from flying over a fence by unbalancing flight. The primaries are cut with sharp scissors close to the coverts on one wing for hens, turkeys and waterfowl. This does not damage the mature feather follicle. Pheasants can have both wings clipped leaving the outer two or three primaries so they can glide down from having climbed a tree, but beware of their primaries being replaced at different times.

Problems/diseases

FEATHERS

Feather pecking: Also caused by overcrowding and/or heat stress if around the tails. Some breeds peck the throat area or around the neck or shoulders. The culprit is often the one with all its feathers. Check that feathers are not being removed by a bird pushing through a wire mesh to get to grass. Remove culprit and only replace when all feathers have regrown. Fitting a bit in the beak (it can still eat and drink but cannot close the beak completely) may be the only solution with a valuable breeding bird, but it may need to be culled if a persistent offender. After weeks of feather growth it only takes minutes for them to be plucked again.

Moulting: Normally takes 3-4 weeks in late summer/early autumn. If longer, check nutrition and mineral content of feed. Calcified seaweed is

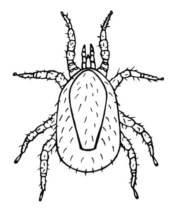

Dermanyssus gallinae *Red mite, actual size about 1mm*

Menopon gallinae *Common fowl louse, lives on skin debris and feathers. Irritant. About 2mm long, yellow.*

useful but slow. It can be fed all year round instead of mixed poultry grit and will improve plumage quality in any case. Stress bars or fret marks will appear on growing feathers following a nutritional crisis (lack of food, bad weather, bullying), but at next moult will disappear if no further insult.

Sexing: Male chickens at age 8-10 weeks will grow pointed, shiny feathers between their shoulder blades (except Silkies)(see page 18).

34

LICE:

Chicken (*Menopon gallinae*): Flat, yellow, fast moving, about ⅛" (2mm) long, usually seen around vent or under wings but move quickly out of the light as feathers are parted. They feed on skin and feather debris. Louse eggs look like granulated sugar clumps attached to base of feathers and need to be removed and burnt. Not life threatening, but better off without them. Dust with Johnson's Flea and Louse Powder (pyrethrum based) or use Ivomec (unlicensed for poultry) drops on shoulder skin. Infestations are worse in autumn and winter.

Waterfowl (*Holomenopon spp*): shaft lice are thin, dark, about ¼"(5mm) long and move quickly deeper into the plumage. Best seen on pale coloured birds. Not usually a problem, but have been associated with Wet Feather (page 36). Ivomec is more toxic to waterfowl than poultry so use with care.

MITES:

Red mite (*Dermanyssus gallinae*) (1mm long, red in colour) live in the hut during daylight and suck the blood of the birds at night causing anaemia, debility and sometimes death. Eggs may have tiny blood spots on the shell and a whitish powder is seen around perch sockets. Carefully blowlamp into crevices or spray with Duramitex (malathion) or dust with pyrethrum based louse powder. Ivomec drops will work when the mites feed. Red mite can live for 6 months without feeding and are then grey and very hungry. Replace felt on the roof with corrugated bitumen or clear corrugated plastic over plyboard to remove dark places for red mite to breed. Vigilance is needed as wild birds will re-infest outdoor poultry at any time - only a ten-day life cycle in warm weather.

Herbal products for control do not seem to be consistent. Some breeders add louse powder to dust baths but this dilutes the chemical and is probably ineffective.

Northern fowl mite (*Ornithonyssus sylvarum*): Similar in size and colour to red mite but spend all the time on the bird causing anaemia and death.

35

Crested breeds are particularly prone and if controlling the mites with pyrethrum based powder, make sure to sprinkle some down the ear canal as this is where they hide. Infested birds have dirty looking patches on them and are depressed. Control is easiest by Ivomec. Reinfestation can occur at any time, but Ivomec is protective for about 4 weeks.

Scaly leg mite (*Cnemidocoptes mutans*): causes intense irritation by burrowing under the scales of the leg, producing at first a whitish film and then mounds of pale yellow debris firmly attached to the leg. The simplest and cheapest cure is to dunk the legs once a week for three weeks in a wide mouthed jar of surgical spirit, or use Ivomec drops as above. Do not be tempted to use the old fashioned remedies of diesel or creosote as these are harmful to the hens. Scales, like feathers, are moulted once a year, so after the crusts have fallen off (do not take them off as the flesh is raw beneath), the legs that were heavily infested may take a year to look something like normal.

Cnemidocoptes gallinae, sometimes called the depluming itch mite, causes feather loss, usually on the neck. It is important to establish if this loss may in fact be due to other birds pulling out feathers or a bird habitually pushing its neck through a fence. If it is this mite, Ivomec may not control it and persistent use of pyrethrum based louse powder may be the answer. Some breeders cull as it is difficult to eradicate. The mite may have a predilection for hard feathered breeds (i.e. Game).

There is an **air sac mite** but it is rare in poultry.

Wet feather: Can be a serious problem in waterfowl as the ability of feathers to remain waterproof is affected. **Shaft lice** have been implicated in this as they cause intense irritation and excessive preening, leading to feather damage. Lack of preening due to sickness can also be a cause. If feathers are soiled by plant oils, spores (sooty mould from osier willow trees will continue to grow on feathers) or chemicals, then wet feather may result. If feather damage is severe, the problem will not resolve until the next moult.

Angel wing: This is a problem of the wing joint, see pages 43 and 46.

The bird on the right with dark feathers has a normal leg. The bird on the left with white feathers has scaly leg leading to raised encrustations and the mites' activities are intensely irritant. It is easier to see the early stages on black legged birds and there is a particular smell which goes with the disease.

The Welsummer bantam is about to be dusted with louse powder. This is easy enough to do with one person if the bird is held first in the normal position with its legs between the fingers of your left hand (if right handed), its body supported by the palm of your hand and your forearm; then put the bird on its back on a solid surface and hold it down with your forearm. This leaves your right hand free to dust under the tail, under the wings, and over the breast. The back and neck can be dusted afterwards, the louse powder (based on pyrethrum) rubbed in with the fingers. If possible, always use light rubber gloves when using any kind of chemical.

37

3 SKELETAL AND LOCOMOTIVE SYSTEM

The diagram shows the skeleton of a chicken; other poultry are similar, with variations in bills or legs. The skull is large, the neck long and very mobile and the bones of the thoracic area fused, with one free thoracic vertebra and then the sacrum and caudal vertebrae. The fused thoracic area is an adaptation for flight which together with the ribs, coracoids and sternum provide the thoracic girdle where the flight or breast muscles are attached. The pelvic area is rigid to provide support for walking and is elongated for egg laying. The one free thoracic vertebra is therefore a point of weakness between two rigid areas. The tail is well supplied with muscles in order to attain a wide range of movement including preening, and the rumpless breeds of chickens are without the uropygium (the parson's nose, within which the bone is the pygostyle). The larger wing bones and most of the vertebral, pelvic and sternal bones are pneumatised (connected to the respiratory system).

If waterfowl are pinioned, it is the metacarpals (carpus)which are removed, up to 7 days old. The legs follow the mammalian system except for the feet and four toes which are variously clawed or webbed. Five breeds of chickens have a fifth toe (Silkie, Sultan, Dorking, Faverolles, Houdan) which is separate from the back toe and angled up the leg, forming the letter 'K' with it. Some Cotunix quail may have similar five toes. Spurs are present on male chickens according to age. They can also occur on some female chickens and the Sumatra has two or even three sets of spurs. Turkeys, ducks and geese do not have spurs and some pheasants have them in both sexes. See page 26 for claw and spur management. The short legged breeds (Scots Dumpies, Japanese) have the shank affected by the dwarfing gene; this gene also carries a lethal factor so some eggs do not hatch; some chicks have the requisite short legs but others have long legs which should not normally be used for breeding.

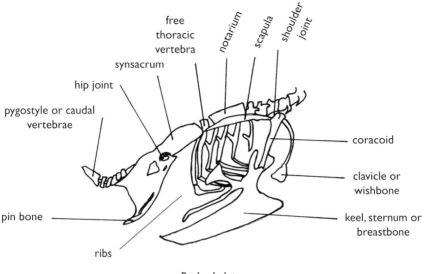

Body skeleton

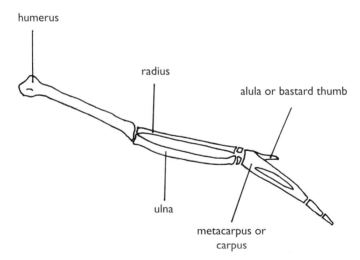

Right wing bones

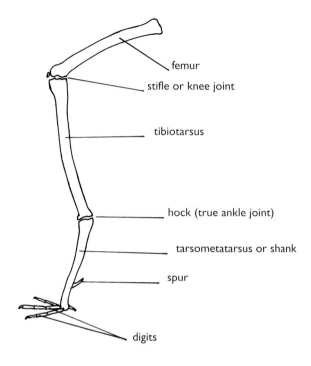

femur

stifle or knee joint

tibiotarsus

hock (true ankle joint)

tarsometatarsus or shank

spur

digits

Left leg bones

The golden pheasant chick has splay leg where the tendons and ligaments are weak. It is worth trying to tie the legs together with soft wool for two days to see if they strengthen. If not, the chick should be culled. Make sure that incubator/ hatcher floors are non-slip and that brooder box floors have a non-slip surface by using an old clean towel or rough kitchen paper for the first few days.

Laysan teal with perosis. The leg is held at an angle and is non weight-bearing. Sometimes in mild cases the tendon can slip in and out and when in, the bird looks normal. Should really be culled as the bird finds it difficult to get around, swims in a circle and is a candidate for being bullied. Check the mineral content of the breeder diet.

The Abyssinian blue-winged goose has angel wing, called 'oar wing' in the USA. On an adult bird there is nothing that can be done to correct the deformity of the carpus, but you can trim back the feathers so they do not look as unsightly. This will have to be done every year after the moult when when all blood has gone out of the quills. On growing waterfowl at the first sign of a drooping wing, tape it up in a natural position for three days (see page 46) and reduce the amount of protein in the feed (feed more wheat than pellets)

The Modern Game and the Modern Langshan have long and upright legs. Never catch or hold a bird by one leg only as the hip will dislocate (see Handling, page 14) Perching in birds is achieved when the bird crouches and tendons in the legs are passively tensed by the flexion of the joints, automatically clamping the digits around the perch. Most chickens walk better than they fly, with their legs being close to the centre of gravity, but some ducks and geese have difficulty walking as their legs are set further back to facilitate swimming. All wildfowl and some domestic waterfowl will readily fly unless pinioned or wing clipped (see page 44). Check when buying birds before they are let out of the box that they are prevented from flying off by having been pinioned or wing clipped.

Broilers tend to have muscles which are all the same blanched colour as they are only 42 days old when slaughtered. Pure breeds and other species vary in the amount of white or red muscle they have depending on purpose: chickens tend to have white breast meat and red muscles in the legs as they do more walking than flying, whereas wild waterfowl and geese have dark red breast meat as these are traditionally the flying muscles.

Problems/diseases

Many skeletal growth problems are nutritional in origin, so check that birds are getting the correct diet for the species. In mixed collections it is not so easy, but if a hopper of grain and a hopper of pellets are provided, the birds will usually feed sensibly.

Splay leg: Chickens and turkeys may be hatched with or develop one or both legs splayed outwards. This may be due to a slippery surface in the incubator or brooder, nutritional deficiency of the parents causing weak tendons or incorrect incubation temperature. In mild cases the legs may be tied together with soft wool for two or three days to allow the tendons to strengthen, but if this does not work the bird should be culled as it will be unable to walk (see page 40).

Slipped tendon or perosis: The gastrocnemius or achilles tendon is displaced at the back of the hock and the lower leg sticks out sideways.

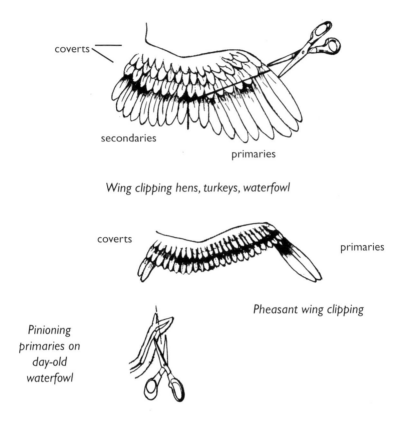

coverts

secondaries

primaries

Wing clipping hens, turkeys, waterfowl

coverts

primaries

Pheasant wing clipping

Pinioning primaries on day-old waterfowl

Small ornamental ducks seem prone to this and it appears when they are growing. Mild cases will be able to get around, but if the bird cannot walk it should be culled. It may be hereditary but has also been linked to a manganese and other mineral deficiency, so ensure correct feeding. Chickens and turkeys may occasionally be affected (see page 41).

Angel wing: Waterfowl are designed to live on grass and grain and are not able to process the high levels of protein normally fed to other poultry, the excess creating skeletal problems and weaknesses. When the primaries start to come through these are full of blood and heavy. If the wing joint has been affected by too much protein it will deform and twist, resulting in the feathers sticking out at an angle which is permanent. If the wing is

The Partridge Wyandotte pullet has one bandy leg, which is a deformity. She may have been born with it, the diet may have been deficient (unlikely if commercial feed has been used) or it may be due to damage to the hock joint. If no other related chicks are affected it is probably just a one-off.

noticed to be drooping on a young bird it may be strapped up with masking tape for a few days and the feed changed to a lower protein one. The weight of the wing is supported and the joint is allowed to develop normally (see page 46).

Certain large domestic geese tend to have angel wing, but it may be that because they are exhibited, breeders try and push them to grow with high protein feed. If the joint has deformed and the feathers are completely through with no blood in the quills, the feathers may be trimmed for aesthetic purposes. The tendency to angel wing may be inherited.

Pinioning: It is illegal to release into the wild non-indigenous species, so most ornamental waterfowl need to be pinioned at a few days old and certainly no more than a week old. There is little blood if it is done at the correct angle and the downies do not seem to be set back by the process. Use sharp scissors and make the cut as in the diagram (p. 43) on one wing only. Have a styptic pencil handy in case of slight bleeding. Some breeders pinion one wing for females and the other side for males, having

The outer toe on the left leg of the Dorking is bent, as is the middle toe. This is the type of deformity which is inherited.

sexed the downies (see page 18) so they can tell the different sexes from a distance. If an ornamental duck suddenly appears with a brood and they are impossible to catch, then wait until just before they can fly - they start to practise with enthusiasm and much flapping - and then clip the primary feathers (see page 33). This will have to be done every year after the moult.

At the next breeding season, try and contain a sitting duck with a ring of very small mesh wire netting when she is due to hatch so the downies can be caught up, or take and artificially incubate the eggs and hand rear the youngsters.

Lameness: In waterfowl this may be due to arthritis in old birds. Meloxicam is useful to ease the discomfort, but culling may be necessary. Hocks seem to be a vulnerable place for infection to settle. This may be caused by *Mycoplasma synoviae* (also see Respiratory, page 71) and needs treating with tylosin. Other bacteria may be involved. Although pure breeds of poultry do not have the very many problems that broilers have in the way of skeletal disorders and leg weakness, there are some infective agents which cause arthritis (joint inflammation), osteomyelitis (bone

45

inflammation) and tenosynovitis (tendon inflammation). These are all painful and can usually be helped with tylosin, lincomycin or spectinomycin. Other disorders are non-infective and may be caused by poor nutrition or inherited. A point of weakness for both infective and non-infective is the T4 vertebra (the free one) between the fused spinal areas and if this is affected, birds may go off their legs (but see Marek's disease, page 95).

Waterfowl tend to go lame on one or both legs if they have intestinal

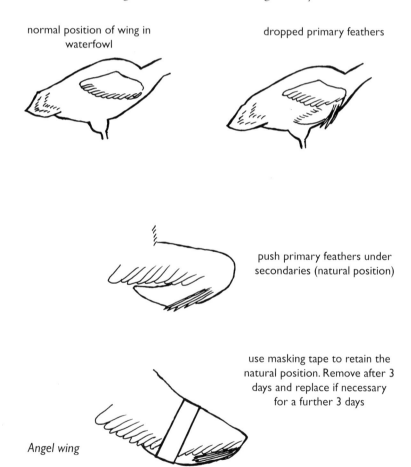

normal position of wing in waterfowl

dropped primary feathers

push primary feathers under secondaries (natural position)

use masking tape to retain the natural position. Remove after 3 days and replace if necessary for a further 3 days

Angel wing

parasites. Treat with Flubenvet or Ivomec. Poultry can go lame if they have kidney disease as the main ischiatic nerve serving the legs passes through the kidneys. Visceral gout causes lameness as kidney failure results in the deposit of urates in the joints (see page 61). Articular gout tends to be hereditary and results in culling.

Turkeys and guinea fowl are susceptible to ionophore toxicity (coccidiostats) and this will result in lameness and maybe death, so check on the feed bag label that it is suitable for these species. Rarely, a bird will sprain a ligament in a leg. They are more usually lame through disease and it is always worth treating lameness as such with medication, as if left without treatment to get better as in a sprain, the disease will only get worse and possibly beyond treatment.

Fractures: Rare in poultry which are properly fed. Most simple leg or wing fractures can be splinted. Fractures elsewhere may be impossible to mend and certainly very expensive.

Deformities: Common inherited deformities deserving culling are roach back (an upward bend in the spine), wry tail (sideways tilt), cow hocks (inward angling of the hocks), dished bill and bent neck in domestic waterfowl. Inwardly bent toes may be inherited or may be due to incorrect incubator temperature - cull anyway, or if the bird is from a valuable strain, breed from it and see if its progeny have the same deformity. A breastbone bent vertically (dented) may be from too narrow perches too young, but if it is bent sideways (S bend) then it is likely to be inherited and should not be bred from.

Rickets: (symptoms are very bowed legs) Rare due to commercial feed containing correct ingredients, but mixing errors at the mill are not unknown. It is prudent to keep a small sample of each batch of feed if on a large scale in case of problems (see Nutritional disorders, page 59)

Hypermetria: High stepping is a central nervous problem, see page 94.

Muscle wastage: If birds are handled regularly, then loss of weight particularly over the breastbone is obvious. This may be caused by intestinal worms (page 55), liver failure or avian TB (page 98). It is not easy to spot loss of weight just by looking as the outline of the bird

The Scots Grey cockerel is showing cow hocks.

remains virtually the same because of the feathers.

4 DIGESTIVE AND EXCRETORY SYSTEMS

Digestive system

'As rare as hens' teeth': an excellent saying, as no birds have them, food being ground up in the gizzard by poultry. Food and plant material is picked up delicately with the beak by chickens, turkeys, quail and guinea fowl who are more sensitive to texture than taste, with the feet being used to scratch the soil surface to disturb insects. Colour vision and shadows help to identify food items. The several breeds of Himalayan pheasants prefer to dig with their powerful beaks and enjoy destroying foliage. The digestive systems are similar in these species, with a certain amount of cellulose digestion by fermentation in the caeca - sections of blind-ended gut. For Nutrition, see Appendix V.

Ducks prefer a more liquid diet, sieving everything through water where possible, using their sensitive bills and fringed tongues, making a lovely mess of mud and destroying the banks of ponds and vegetation in their endless search for food. Geese and muscovy ducks are grazers with a very short gut transit time but will nibble the bark off trees or unprotected wood on fences or huts given a chance. Short, sweet, young grass is preferred by all poultry and old fibrous grass can impact with fatal results. Waterfowl also digest plant material in their caeca.

The tongue is muscular and the hard palate ridged to help hold food. The choana is a horizontal opening in the hard palate connecting the mouth to the nasal cavity; it reflexively closes during swallowing. Salivary glands are both in the hard palate and on the floor of the mouth. All poultry drink by taking a mouthful of water and then tipping their heads up to swallow, unlike pigeons which suck water in in a continuous flow. There is a large laryngeal mound at the back of the tongue with a rough surface which helps with swallowing and the glottis closes to prevent

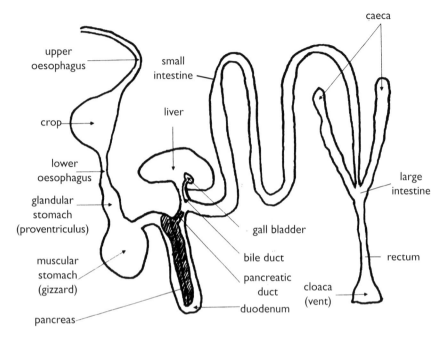

The digestive system of a hen

food entering the trachea. The oesophagus is capable of great distension, mucus glands producing lubricant for the food, which is stored in an enlarged section - the crop - in poultry, where the food undergoes softening and swelling. Geese do not have such a large crop, but store food in the same area. When exhibiting, the desired outline of a bird can easily be spoiled by food bulging in its crop.

The stomach (proventriculus) provides the main chemical digestion of food with gastric glands opening into it. The strongly muscular gizzard provides the main physical digestion of food with ingested grit being used to grind it, plus a low pH (acid) environment, which helps to break the food down. Food passes between stomach and gizzard and gizzard and stomach several times before entering the duodenum as a mush, ready for further digestion and absorption. It is vital that mixed poultry grit (oystershell and insoluble grit) is provided once birds are 10 weeks old or being fed whole grain, whichever is the earlier, in order for the gizzard to develop properly. The food then travels through the intestines where protrusions called villi have absorptive surfaces for the various constituents of feed to be absorbed into the bloodstream: amino acids, carbohydrates, glucose, minerals and fats.

The paired caeca are where cellulose breakdown takes place via bacterial fermentation. Large intestine contents are voided into the rectum and then the cloaca. The caeca void their contents about every tenth dropping and are usually dark brown and glutinous, depending on what the bird has been eating. Normal faeces in hens are firm, brown and with a white tip which is the urates (see Excretory system, below). Waterfowl faeces are less firm, usually dark green with pale green or white urates.

The dark red liver has two lobes, the right is larger than the left. Nutrients from the gut are brought here via the blood and any detoxification necessary takes place. Re-forming of amino acids into proteins which the body can use, energy storage, storage of vitamin A and iron are other functions of the liver, plus the formation of fat which goes to the ova in the blood to create yolk. The gall bladder, if accidentally punctured when eviscerating a carcase, will bitterly taint the meat. Good nutrition is obtained by using commercial feed plus access to herbage.

Excretory system

The kidneys lie within the protection of the bony synsacrum. The spinal nerves of the lumbar plexus and the sacral plexus pass through the kidneys, serving mainly the legs and tail. Birds excrete semi-solid urates (mammals excrete liquid urine), the ureter opening into the urodeum and these are stored in the rectum until voided with faeces. There is no bladder or urethra, unlike mammals.

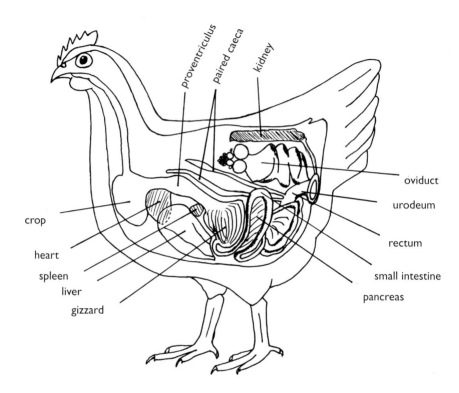

proventriculus
paired caeca
kidney
oviduct
urodeum
crop
rectum
heart
spleen
small intestine
liver
pancreas
gizzard

Digestive system and internal organs

Problems/diseases

Choking: Birds can choke on grain or any other food. If you are lucky and see them do it it may be possible to remove the piece by gently squeezing the bird around the body (the Heimlich manoeuvre), but mostly a bird is found dead in good condition. It is useful to open up any bird found dead when a mechanical cause of death may be discovered.

Dropped tongue: This seems to be a particular problem of certain strains of Toulouse geese. The tongue gets trapped in the sagging, fleshy floor of the mouth and food gets trapped with it. Feeding is restricted and

52

infection may set in. The floor of the mouth needs to be stitched by a veterinary surgeon so that it is the correct shape. It usually happens to the best looking birds, so it is tempting to breed from them and perpetrate the fault.

Sour crop (thrush): The yeast *Candida albicans* can proliferate if oral antibiotic therapy has been used, or if there is a deficiency of Vitamin A (unlikely in outdoor birds). There is a pungent sour smell from the crop and the bird is lethargic. Treat orally with ketoconazole or nystatin.

Seaducks (eiders, scoters, longtailed ducks) are prone to *Candida* infection if they do not have access to salt water as their nasal salt glands atrophy (salt appears to inhibit yeasts, but only seaducks can cope with salt water).

Crop impaction: Sometimes known as crop binding. Long stemmy grass is usually the culprit. This cannot physically pass on down the digestive tract and the bird stops eating. The crop will feel doughy. In mild or early cases the mass may be softened by pouring liquid paraffin down the throat and gently squeezed out through the mouth with the bird upside down, making sure that regular breaks are taken to allow the bird to breathe. In severe cases the crop may need to be opened up by a veterinary surgeon to remove the mass. Birds recover quite well, but the risk is there for it to happen again as the muscles of the crop have been distorted. If left alone, the bird will starve.

Pendulous crop: The crop appears to be hanging below the normal outline of the bird. This is related to crop binding, but the muscles of the crop weaken and are unable to push the food through to the proventriculus. In early cases, the bird should be caged with just water and put onto feed very gradually after a few days. Again, the crop may be gently milked out, but as the muscles are damaged, it is likely to happen again. When handling birds at night their crops should be full especially to get them through the long winter nights, and it is usually gone by the morning. Weak muscles can be caused by lead or zinc poisoning (see page 100) or a lack of available calcium (see page 60).

Impacted gizzard: A hunched up, non feeding, non defecating bird may have an impacted gizzard. This is caused by either a lack of grit or eating of inappropriate material such as shavings or sand. Cage the bird with just water and give liquid paraffin using a syringe, introducing it into the side of the mouth, but the condition can be fatal. Lead poisoning can cause gizzard or gut impaction as the muscles are paralysed (see page 100)

DIARRHOEA (A) PARASITIC:

The bird or birds may be hunched up, not eating, thin. A parasitic egg count may be done on the faeces, but treatment for either worms or protozoa would probably be the speedy first action.

Coccidia: the birds will get an immunity to coccidia, but the very young and the debilitated are at risk and immunity will wane if the challenge disappears. There are 7 types in hens, 5 in turkeys, 3 in geese, 1 in ducks, 3 in pheasants, 1 in quail and 2 in guinea fowl. They tend to be species specific and not all are pathogenic. In hens they are most important economically and are usually controlled by low levels of coccidiostats (coccidia inhibitors, not killers) in the feed so that the birds are constantly exposed to a small challenge. It takes only 7 days for the oocysts (coccidia eggs) to be ingested by the hen, multiply to millions in the wall of the intestine and be excreted to infect the next birds. The oocysts can survive for years if kept damp, not exposed to frost or over 56°C and most disinfectants are not effective. It may be assumed that any birds reared on litter will be infected. Any batch of youngsters especially on damp litter which stop eating, look hunched and maybe have blood and/or mucus in their loose faeces should be treated with Baycox in the water. Unfortunately this is very expensive for the small flock as the container is large. Amprolium is no longer licensed for poultry but is still licensed for pheasants. Amprol plus ethopabate (Proleth) may be made up to a veterinary surgeon's specification and added to the water. See Diseases Chart, page 105.

There is a vaccination, Paracox, and this will be the route in the future, but it is still expensive and not packaged for the smaller user. Some breeds may be genetically resistant to coccidia such as the Fayoumi. Ivomec is not supposed to control coccidia, but in practice it does seem to sometimes.

Histomonas: this is a protozoa affecting the liver in turkeys, pheasants, quail, peacocks and guinea fowl manifesting with bright yellow diarrhoea, the disease also being known as blackhead. The intermediate host of this protozoa is the heterakis intestinal worm carried by chickens, hence the old adage never to keep turkeys and chickens together. If hens are wormed, then the incidence of blackhead is reduced. Action needs to be taken speedily when yellow diarrhoea is seen as birds can die in a couple of days. Treatment is with dimetridazole (Emtryl) in the water. Most turkey feed has Emtryl in it as a preventative, but occasionally if turkeys are stressed, they can still contract the disease, so it is important to keep a small amount of Emtryl powder in the medicine cupboard.

Hexamita: a protozoal commensal (normal inhabitant) of the gut but can cause diarrhoea and unthriftiness in turkey and pheasant poults. Treatment is with Emtryl.

Trichomonas: oral canker in hens, turkeys, pheasants caused by a protozoa. A white to pale yellow cheesy substance appears in the mouth and throat. It is always worth checking a new purchase for this by opening the mouth. Treatment is with Emtryl but takes a long time to resolve.

Helminths: many types of pathogenic parasites can be present throughout the bird (for gapeworm, see Respiratory, page 67) but with the advent of Flubenvet (an anthelmintic powder either added in feed by the mill or added by the breeder to feed), none of them should be a problem. The usual ones are gapeworm, capillaria, heterakis, ascarids, trichostrongyles, tapeworm, fluke and gizzard worm. If using Ivomec against ectoparasites (external), some endoparasites (internal) will be dealt with, but not tapeworm or fluke, so it is better to use Flubenvet. If selling eggs for human consumption, Flubenvet may be used without withdrawal provided it is below 30 ppm, but this negates the effect against tapeworm.

Goslings are susceptible to gizzard worm, going off their legs and then dying. Treat with Flubenvet at the first signs. It is a good idea to worm all stock twice a year outside the breeding season in any case. This should avoid the situation where a bird is so full of worms that either it gets impacted, or, when the worms are killed, the toxins they release kill

The liver of a turkey with blackhead. Not everyone will want to open up a dead bird, but it can be a useful exercise.

the bird. Most intestinal worms have earthworms or insects as a transport host and wild birds are also carriers so outdoor birds are always at risk although a certain amount of immunity develops. Stress can alter the delicate balance and allow the intestinal worms to proliferate. Try and rotate heavily grazed areas to avoid a build up of endoparasites. Most vets do not stock Flubenvet and will use Panacur. This is only a partial solution as it is effective against only half of the types of potential parasites. Flubenvet is easily obtainable from gamekeeper suppliers.

DIARRHOEA (B) INFECTIOUS:

Salmonellas of many types are present in a large number of wild and domestic birds, only some of which are infective to humans (zoonotic). *Salmonella pullorum* is specific to hens, turkeys and pheasants and can cause a white diarrhoea and unthriftiness. It used to be known as bacillary white diarrhoea (BWD) and there is an agglutination blood test which has to be undertaken for export purposes. It is not as common as it was as carriers (it is passed on through the egg) can be identified by the blood test and culled. Signs can be many dead chicks in shell or deaths shortly after hatching, or white faeces stuck to vent feathers and poor growth with pale combs in older birds. The bacteria is also spread in the incubator

The position of the head and neck in the young dead bird is typical of duck viral hepatitis.

and rearing units. Flocks in the MAFF Poultry Health Scheme are free of *pullorum* disease due to compulsory use of the blood test, but many backyard flocks still have it, with the organism surviving in the environment for many months. Treatment is best by culling as any treated birds are liable to be carriers.

Salmonella gallinarum causes fowl typhoid in all types of poultry, usually seen in growers or adults, the symptoms being birds off their food, yellow diarrhoea, ruffled feathers, pale comb and general loss of condition. It is not as common as it was due to the fact that the blood test for *S. pullorum* will denote carriers. Carriers may remain after treatment, so culling is the best option.

Salmonella typhimurium and *S. enteritidis* are the ones that are zoonotic. It is also possible for humans to infect poultry with salmonella! These organisms appear in the birds at a very young age with pasted up vents and a strong smell, ruffled feathers, drooping wings and a high death rate. Faecal contamination of the hatching egg is a common source of salmonella infection, so washing all hatching eggs in Virkon (water warmer than the eggs) is a sensible precaution. Vaccination is possible. Rats and mice are carriers of salmonella, so vermin control is important.

Wild birds also carry it, especially flocks of starlings, jackdaws, rooks or bluetits. Keep pelleted feed in the hen hut to avoid this and only feed enough grain outside that the birds can eat in a short time. Following on from the salmonella scare in the late 1980s, laying flocks had to be tested for salmonella, but this has since been rescinded. Current regulations concerning the sale of eggs can be obtained by contacting the local MAFF office (in telephone directories under Agriculture, Ministry of).

E. coli: These bacteria are normal inhabitants of the digestive tracts of mammals and birds. In stressful conditions, some strains can cause disease and overcrowded chicks around 4 weeks old are susceptible to colibacillosis with a sharp drop in food consumption followed by listlessness and ruffled feathers. Breathing is laboured and rapid but few birds die. They are adversely affected, however, and do not grow well. The organism survives well in dust and chicks produce an enormous amount of this. Infection is more likely if *Mycoplasma* (see page 69) is present. Amoxicillin in the water is useful as a treatment. *Campylobacter jejuni* has been implicated in enteric disease of poultry, but is also a commensal. It is zoonotic.

Streptococcosis: A cause of diarrhoea, but also of abscesses.

Rotavirus: Occasionally in chicks and turkeys but more often in pheasant poults causing enteritis and a malabsorption-type diarrhoea due to intestinal villi being destroyed (the place of absorption in the intestine). Healthy intestine will repair itself in three days under normal wear and tear. Once the villi are destroyed by the virus however, secondary infections of opportunistic bacteria such as *E. coli* will invade the cells. Young chickens and young pheasants seem susceptible to this virus and the stress of change is a predisposing factor. Several stressors in a short space of time have a cumulative effect, so gradual changes are less of a problem. Because this is a malabsorption syndrome, the birds weaken quickly, do not have the strength to find food and thus get weaker and die. Prevention is the best method of control with gradual changes of feed, etc., plus good feed and proper shelter.

Duck viral enteritis: Also known as duck plague, caused by a herpes virus and confined to ducks, geese and swans, mostly in late spring and early summer. The most susceptible species are mallard, muscovy, sheldgeese and shelducks. Dead birds are found in good condition but often with their heads over their backs and a raised tail. Sick birds may have blood coming from the vent and a bloody nasal discharge with a hypersensitivity to light. Males may have a prolapsed penis. There are small haemorrhages throughout the body, but especially in the heart. Prevention is by excluding free-flying feral waterfowl from the collection or by vaccination at 4 weeks when there is no sign of disease (Intervet). If disease is present, healthy birds may be vaccinated to limit the spread. Clinically affected birds should be culled.

Duck viral hepatitis: Birds less than 4 weeks die with heads back. Breeding females can be vaccinated, but affected birds are doomed. Other viruses affect chickens, turkeys and waterfowl causing enteritis, but they are unusual in extensive, outdoor birds. Viruses cannot be treated except by prevention by vaccination. Sometimes nursing and the control of secondary bacterial infections can be a help, but birds if they do recover are usually unthrifty due to the damage caused.

DIARRHOEA (C) DIETARY. Excess cabbage may cause diarrhoea.

Peritonitis: Usually caused by a small piece of sharp wire which penetrates the gut causing septicaemia. Mostly in waterfowl as they tend to grubble and dig, but usually fatal. Prevention is by collecting nails, staples, wire etc, if fencing, and checking that wire netting is not disintegrating through age, damage or rust.

Nutritional disorders: These may be caused by a dietary insufficiency, inhibition of absorption, a metabolic abnormality or starvation by being bullied away from the feed. Fat-soluble vitamins (A & E) are involved with membranes, water-soluble vitamins with enzyme systems and minerals with bone growth and egg production. Commercial feeds contain all necessary nutrients as a huge amount of research has gone into poultry nutrition, so a simple deficiency is rare. If parent stock is well fed, then chicks and downies will hatch with a good source of nutrients in the yolk and have a good start in life.

Vitamin A deficiency is unusual in outdoor birds with access to grass and on commercial feed, but many chickens and ducks are kept on too small an area which rapidly becomes bare of all vegetation. They become prone to infections in the mouth and throat plus eye infections, are generally weak and stop laying. A supplement formulated for birds should help, and make sure that birds have access to grass; excess levels of Vitamin A are toxic, so supplementation should be used with care.

Vitamin E functions as an antioxidant and deficiency can cause early embryo death, crazy chick disease (encephalomalacia), heart disease and nutritional muscular dystrophy which usually occurs with blood leakage under the skin on the breast and under the wings. Commercial feed normally contains sufficient Vitamin E. Low levels of this vitamin are implicated in capture myopathy, usually manifested in waterfowl after transportation. Spontaneous recovery occurs once the bird eats again.

Vitamin K is involved in blood coagulation and may be affected if antibacterial drugs are antagonistic (counteract the action) - the sulpha drugs appear to be the main antagonists.

B Vitamins: deficiencies tend to manifest as skin disorders or poor hatchability, but the main B Vitamin which shows clinical signs at marginally low levels is B2 (riboflavin). Curly toe paralysis with the toes clenched (distinguish from bent toes, page 47) plus clubbed down (where the down feathers are fluffy but 'clubbed' at the ends, forming a coiled structure) is a classic symptom in chicks, but again, unusual with commercial feed. Deficiency in adults results in embryo deaths in mid and late incubation (dead-in-shell). This vitamin is also needed for melanin production in black coloured birds.

Calcium and phosphorus ratio in feed should be 2:1. Calcium is vital throughout all body cells for efficient function, not just in bones and phosphorus is important in protein synthesis and carbohydrate metabolism. Deficiency shows in depleted growth of the skeleton and rickets (bowed leg bones) in young birds. It is said young birds are more prone to feather pecking with a calcium deficiency, but excess heat and stress are also implicated. Thin or soft shelled eggs is a sign in laying birds, but it is normal for the hen to use calcium from her bones for shell formation. Mash feed can result in a deficiency due to the heavier mineral particles settling out. Stress can make calcium unavailable temporarily, see egg bound page 83. Calcium and phosphorus supplementation is best done in a naturally balanced form such as calcified seaweed in order to maintain the optimum ratio, plus other minerals such as iodine. Excess calcium will lead to kidney failure.

Vitamin D starts out as a steroid (cholesterol) and is converted by ultraviolet light to the vitamin. Birds sunbathe with wings and legs outstretched. Oil from the preen gland has a cholesterol component and thus contributes slightly to vitamin D production once on the feathers. It is essential for calcium transport in the blood. Outdoor birds with access to sunlight should not have a deficiency, neither should birds with limited outside access, such as on an aviary system and sharing a piece of grass every few days in rotation. Commercial feed is supplemented with vitamin D_3(the active version).

Sodium chloride: salt is added to all rations, but deficiency will depress egg production and increase cannibalism. Excess will cause convulsions and kidney damage.

Zinc is an essential trace element affecting growth, reproduction, skin and feathers. High calcium levels will reduce availability. In excess it is very toxic and damaged galvanised drinkers and feeders can produce toxicity resulting in weakness, weight loss and convulsions. Treatment is with sodium calciumedetate (see lead poisoning, page 100).

Excess protein can result in angel wing (see page 46)

Fatty liver syndrome: usually occurs with old, obese birds which no longer take exercise or lay eggs. The friable liver haemorrhages and birds will die, especially in hot weather.

Excretory problems/diseases

Hereditary: Bird will be a poor doer. May be atrophy or only one kidney.
Visceral gout: Bird will be off feed, depressed and a poor doer. This is a sequel to renal failure and is where urate crystals are deposited on the

surfaces of the abdominal viscera and on the synovial membranes of joints (do not confuse with articular gout, page 47). Ureters may be impacted.

Kidney diseases

Neprosis: bird will be a poor doer, and will appear depressed. Kidney damage mostly by poisons (see Poisons, page 100).

Nephritis: symptom is general unthriftiness. Kidney inflammation caused by mycoplasma (page 60), infectious bronchitis (page 71), Gumboro (page 89). As the nerves of the legs course through the kidneys, lameness can occur.

Nutritional problems: Vitamin A deficiency: young birds on a vitamin A deficient diet may be depressed, off their food, and die within 3 weeks with visceral gout and impacted ureters due to the lining of the ureters becoming thickened and a lower production of mucus, so the urates cannot pass through.

Salt poisoning: young birds with excess sodium in the feed suffer severe renal damage. If potassium is added to the diet, the birds should recover. Water deprivation may not lead to salt poisoning, but birds can survive only a short time without water. Clean water helps prevent kidney and other diseases.

Stones (Uroliths): Bird will be off feed, depressed and unwilling to move. Excess calcium causes kidney failure and stones in the ureters. Infectious bronchitis and water deprivation can also cause these.

5 RESPIRATORY SYSTEM

Eyes

These are included here as, due to the anatomy of a bird, the eyes tend to be affected by respiratory problems. Hens may not have teeth, but all birds have small bones (ossicles) in their eyes for strength and muscle attachment. Birds are intensely visual and have a large eye in relation to the size of the head. Most poultry have binocular vision but can also move each eye independently; they will tip the head sideways to look at an aeroplane or bird in the sky (possible predator) with one eye, which looks comical but is most effective and necessary in a prey species. Waterfowl have specially adapted lenses so they can see underwater and all birds see colour including part of the ultraviolet spectrum. Hens are attracted by red, hence the colour of drinker and feeder bases, but pheasants prefer yellow.

Hens do not see well at night and thus prefer to go to safe roost in daylight whereas waterfowl see quite well at night (consider migration), thus they do not like going indoors to bed. Fortunately domestic ducks and geese are trainable, drivable and creatures of habit, but they will get spooked by moonlight and shadows.

In order to close the eye, the bottom lid comes up to meet the top. This usually only happens when the bird is asleep. In order to blink, the third eyelid (nictitating membrane) moves from front to back over the surface of the eye. This can sometimes be seen in photographs and happens at roughly two-second intervals. The pupil is round and has a fast reaction so that small movement (insects) can be spotted more easily. Waterfowl are capable of sleeping with one eye and one half of the brain at a time, most useful as a survival tactic in a prey species. Perhaps this is one reason why geese are such good watchdogs.

Problems/diseases

Ammonia blindness: In overcrowded and dirty conditions conjunctivitis or even blindness can occur if ammonia levels are high - if you can smell ammonia then the levels are probably too high. Low levels of ventilation in winter will exacerbate the problem. Even if conditions are improved, the sensitive cornea may not recover.

Foreign bodies: Does not normally seem to be a problem, but any inflamed or weeping eye should be inspected for foreign bodies.

Sinusitis: Swellings here can press on the eye and ultimately cause blindness and/or infection (see Mycoplasma, page 71)

Trauma: A traumatised eye is best left to heal with antibiotic cover and without being removed, as removal causes many problems due to the small area and intimate position with the brain. Birds cope well if blind in one eye but have serious problems if blind in both and should be culled.

Treatment: Usually with antibiotics either in the water or injected. Eye drops are difficult to administer due to the nictitating membrane, but some vaccinations are given this way.

Respiratory system

Once the very different avian (compared to mammal) respiratory system is understood, it is easier to prevent disease (see page 70). There is a keratinised flap of skin (operculum) at the top of the nostrils in poultry which effectively narrows the opening. The inside of the nasal passages is very convoluted not, as in mammals, to increase the smelling area, but to act as a heat exchanger and avoid excess water loss in hot, dry conditions. If sufficient thermoregulation cannot be achieved via the nasal passages, poultry will pant and also flutter the throat to keep cool (gular flutter). Air is filtered, warmed and hydrated on inspiration, but the passage is narrow and very quickly gets blocked by inflammation. Waterfowl have a slightly less complicated nasal area, without the operculum, but seaducks have a salt gland so that they can drink sea water and excrete the salt through this gland. Poultry and waterfowl do not need a good sense of smell - it has been compared to that of humans

64

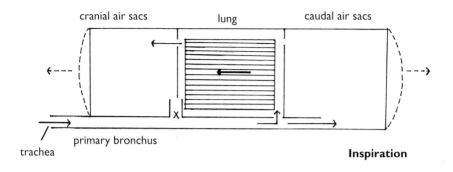

Inspiration

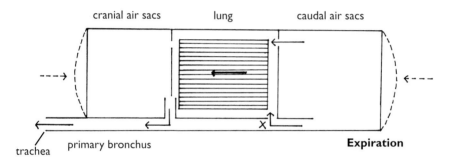

Expiration

Avian lungs and how they work

On inspiration (top diagram) *the cranial and caudal air sacs expand. Outside air flows to the caudal sacs through the primary bronchus and lung air flows into the cranial sacs.*

On expiration (bottom diagram) *air from the caudal sacs flows into the lungs and air from the cranial sacs is exhaled through the trachea. Air does not flow significantly where X is placed. Thus air flows through the lungs in one direction only on both inspiration and expiration. The ribs are hinged and mobile in order to expand sufficiently. The whole system is a high velocity, low pressure system and hinges on aerodynamic flow patterns, with the air sacs playing a vital part.*

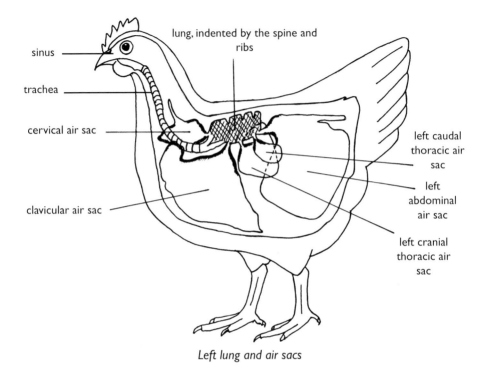

sinus

trachea

cervical air sac

clavicular air sac

lung, indented by the spine and ribs

left caudal thoracic air sac

left abdominal air sac

left cranial thoracic air sac

Left lung and air sacs

- their other senses being better developed. The sinuses are spacious triangular cavities under the skin just in front of each eye and the swelling of one or both of these is often an early sign of respiratory disease. Foam in the corner of the eye is probably the earliest sign.

The trachea is long, due to the long neck, wider than in a mammal of comparable size and the rate of breathing is slower (by one third) to compensate for extra dead space (the air left in the system after expiration and not involved in gas exchange) plus a four times greater tidal volume (the amount of gas passing in and out of the lungs in each respiratory cycle). The cartilage rings which keep the trachea open are a complete circle and slightly overlap each other. In swans there is an excavation in the sternum to accommodate the coils of the very long trachea.

The syrinx is the voicebox, not the larynx as in mammals, and is usually positioned at the end of the trachea nearest the lungs. Songbirds have five pairs of syringeal muscles, poultry usually only one. Waterfowl have a slightly different arrangement, presumably to accommodate a slightly different voice. The lungs are dorsally placed, protected by the spine and ribs with which they are intimately involved as they do not expand, unlike mammalian lungs. Each lung is small, flattened and although the same weight as in a comparable mammal, is 25% smaller but with 20% greater surface area. This is due to the intricate arrangement of small bronchi (airways) which are open at both ends, unlike mammals' which have blind-ended alveoli (sacs where gas exchange takes place). The larger surface area means more efficient gas exchange with the myriad of air capillaries being surrounded by blood capillaries.

The open-ended small bronchi has the effect that air needs to flow only in one direction and does so both on inspiration and expiration (with mammals, they are blind ended, and so air must flow in 2 directions, in and out). This is achieved due to the presence of air sacs which act as short-term storage of air for each respiratory cycle. The air sacs are not involved in gas exchange and there are 8 in the chicken (2 pairs fused) and 7 in the turkey, the cranial ones being adapted to produce the 'poomph' of the displaying male. There is no diaphragm. The caudal air sacs get fresh air on inspiration, air moves through the lungs, and the cranial air sacs get air from the lungs after gas exchange has taken place. On expiration, air flows to the lungs from the caudal air sacs, through the lungs and the cranial air sac contents are exhaled. The air sacs are connected to the lungs both directly to a secondary bronchus and indirectly by branching extensively with the small bronchi; they are also connected to pneumatised bones: the sternum, humerus, cervical and thoracic vertebrae, coracoid, ribs, synsacrum and pelvis. From this is it clear that any infection in the lungs quickly goes throughout the body of the bird and makes it much more difficult to treat if further down the line than in the early stages.

The sinuses on this Nebraskan spotted turkey hen are swollen with a mycoplasma infection. Turkey sinuses are larger than chickens' so it is easier to see on a turkey, but the first signs of sneezing and foam in the eye should alert you to start treatment. If left, the bird will die as it will not ultimately be able to breathe.

Problems/diseases

Crowing: Cockerels will crow no matter what. There is no method of physically silencing them, but putting them in a dark box overnight to reduce the sound and frequency will often placate unhappy neighbours.

Blocked nasal openings: This can sometimes happen with chronic respiratory problems. A discharge accumulates and hardens at the nasal opening. It is possible to remove this carefully, remembering that some species have a sensitive operculum which needs to remain.

Nasal leeches: Waterfowl are prone to these, but they can easily be cleared with ivermectin (200mcg/kg bodyweight).

Sinusitis: In poultry, swollen sinuses are usually due to mycoplasma infection. Tylosin should keep this under control but will sometimes need several injections if the sinus is filled with solid material. Lancing is not

A White Sussex with gapeworm, trying hard to breathe adequately. The same symptoms may be seen in Infectious Bronchitis. If Flubenvet has recently been used for worming, then suspect IB.

generally effective. In waterfowl the cause can be mycoplasma or pseudomonas bacteria: the sinus is usually swollen with fluid and needs lancing, milking out and then flushing with Baytril 2.5% through the nostril for several days, remembering to hold closed the opposite nostril while flushing as the nasal septum (dividing partition) is not complete in waterfowl. It needs 5ml for a small duck such as teal up to 30ml daily for a large swan.

Ammonia: Ammonia from litter in overcrowded or poorly ventilated areas is immunosuppressive and stops the cilia from working effectively. Cilia are small hairs in the trachea of birds and mammals which are always moving a layer of mucus containing trapped particles, dust or pathogens, towards the oesophagus to be swallowed and deactivated by stomach acid. Ammonia and smoke are two substances which paralyse cilia, thus leaving the animal open to infection.

Gapeworm: These inhabit the trachea of non-aquatic birds with male and female worm permanently linked in a Y shape. Infected birds will cough, snick or gasp for breath. Gapeworm eggs are coughed up, swallowed and voided with the faeces to continue the life cycle as larvae in earthworms where they may survive for years until either wild birds or domestic ones continue the cycle. The eggs can survive in the soil for nine months, so try and rotate susceptible areas. Flubenvet in the feed is the treatment for all poultry and pheasants and on a regular basis (2 or 3 times a year, outside the breeding season) should prevent serious infestation. Pheasant poults seem particularly prone to gapeworm and waterfowl can suffer from a different tracheal worm, but signs and treatment are the same.

Aspergillus fungus: All classes of poultry are susceptible; diving and seaducks are the most susceptible of waterfowl, especially if they never have salt water. It is a very difficult disease to treat successfully as there are few early symptoms and once spread throughout the air sacs, lungs, bones and abdomen, when it causes distressed breathing, it may well be too late. Avoid mouldy hay or straw or rotting or decaying vegetable matter as it is the spores of the fungus which are inhaled. Most healthy unstressed birds will cope with a low level of infection, but can die suddenly under stress. It is also passed on through the egg. Antifungal agents such as itraconazole are successful if the disease is caught early enough. This disease is zoonotic, being known in humans as Farmer's Lung.

Air sacculitis: This is a general term covering several air sac diseases in all poultry ranging from parasitic (air sac mites: mainly a problem in very small adult birds) to chlamydia to aspergillosis.

Air sac leakage: This subcutaneous emphysema sometimes occurs; it is usually the cervical air sac leaking and air appears under the skin locally or all over, making the bird look like a balloon caricature. If this does not resolve in a few days, a nick can be made in the skin to let the air out. Unless a longer lasting hole is made in the skin by a vet, thus allowing the air sac wall to heal, the condition will recur, creating an uncomfortable condition for the bird.

Mycoplasma: Used to be known as roup in the old poultry books as chronic disease will cause rattling in the trachea. Mycoplasmas not only cause respiratory disease themselves, they associate with other pathogens such as *E. coli* and debilitate the bird sufficiently that any passing disease will take hold. Foam in the corner of the eye is an early sign, followed by swollen sinuses and rattly breathing. Tylosin (Tylan 200) as an injection will keep the disease under control, but it will only be cured by culling. Some commercial flocks are free of it, but it is carried by wild birds and is very contagious - exhibiting is a prime time to come home with it. It is also carried on clothing, hands and boots for several hours. As long as birds are injected with tylosin at the first signs it does not become a problem. If your flock has mycoplasma (as most backyard flocks do) it may be sensible to inject on purchase of birds from elsewhere. Chicken and turkey mycoplasmas will infect each other, but other species have their own types. *Mycoplasma gallisepticum* is the respiratory organism but it can also settle in the kidneys. *M. synoviae* affects joints making them swell and the bird lame.

Infectious bronchitis (IB): This is a virus and causes respiratory disease and kidney damage in young poultry, plus oviduct infection with depressed egg production in layers and poor shell quality, often wrinkled. Odd birds laying wrinkled eggs may be carriers and should be culled. It is not sensible to set for hatching any egg which is less than a good shape. Vaccination has not proved to give particularly good control in outdoor birds, but if mycoplasma can be controlled, this reduces the opportunity for the virus to invade. The signs of IB are similar to mycoplasma, but the spread of infection of IB is 1-3 days throughout a flock: mycoplasma tends to affect fewer birds. Commercial flocks vaccinate against IB and Newcastle disease (see page 97) at the same time (Intervet) and if there is a problem in your area it is possible to do this to try and protect your birds.

Avian influenza: First defined in 1878 and linked to mammalian influenza viruses, all of which have the ability to mutate (compare with human strains). Wild birds including wild waterfowl are implicated in

The hock joint on the left is infected with Mycoplasma synoviae *and the bird would probably be lame.*

Severely swollen sinus obscuring the eye on a White Orpington, probably due to Mycoplasma gallisepticum. *If a bird or flock is infected, control measures such as Tylan (preferably injectable) will prevent the infection from progressing to this stage where the bird is unlikely to recover fully, even with treatment.*

Infectious Bronchitis (IB) can make chicks gasp for breath. It is unusual for Mycoplasma gallisepticum or gapeworm to affect chicks this badly this young.

its spread through oral and faecal contact and it is a notifiable disease (a legal obligation to tell the police or MAFF if it is suspected). It seems to spread readily between pigs, humans and turkeys, but vaccination is only recommended in susceptible geographical areas e.g. Minnesota (USA), Norfolk (UK), both of which are on migratory waterfowl routes. Clinical signs are sudden death, sudden stopping of egg laying in a flock, respiratory signs, sinusitis, swelling of the face, haemorrhage of the head and wattles and diarrhoea: these signs are not a definitive diagnosis in themselves, a laboratory test (ELISA) is needed for confirmation. Liaise with your vet for current practices.

Pasteurella anatipestifer: Ducklings gasp and have an ocular discharge with sudden death. Symptoms can appear three days after a stressful occurrence. A vaccination is available, and treatment with lincomycin is sometimes successful.

Pasteurella multocida: This bacteria is a commensal in many mammals but not generally in poultry or wild birds. Rats are a known infective source. The disease is known as fowl cholera and symptoms include respiratory distress, lameness, lethargy and swollen wattles. Antibiotics including sulphonamides are effective and there is also a vaccine.

Chlamydia: Also known as psittacosis or ornithosis, this is a potentially dangerous zoonotic disease as it first appears in humans as pneumonia or abortion in women. Make sure your doctor knows you keep birds to avoid misdiagnosis which could be fatal. Infection in birds can cause ocular and nasal discharge and distressed breathing. It is confirmed by laboratory (ELISA) test. Most people think it can only be caught from parrots, but turkeys, ducks and pigeons have also been implicated, together with sheep. It is a difficult organism to treat (usually tetracycline long term) as it has as part of its life cycle a stage which hides inside cells, therefore no antibacterials can reach it.

Infectious laryngotracheitis (ILT): Caused by a herpes virus and mainly affecting male, heavy breed chickens. Symptoms are a nasal discharge, gasping and tracheal plugs of mucus which can cause death. Mycoplasma, IB, Vitamin A deficiency and ammonia will predispose to more severe disease plus there is a carrier state. No treatment as this is a virus, so best to cull or destock.

6 REPRODUCTIVE SYSTEM

Birds have a different chromosomal organisation from mammals in that the male in birds is XX, the female XY, and the female determines the sex of the progeny. Birds are photoperiodic, that is they come into breeding condition after decreasing day length followed by increasing day length. Most poultry seem to be able to breed all year round, but moulting and winter cramps their style a little. Waterfowl are most fertile in the spring, although they choose their mates during the winter.

The study of sex-linkage through plumage in chickens was started in the 1930s. It can be done either through colour or pattern. For example if a male Rhode Island Red (genetically gold) is mated to a female Light Sussex (genetically silver) then all the progeny will be gold females and silver males. This is why most commercial (battery) laying hens are brown, as this was the original cross, the cockerels being white. It does not work the other way round. With patterns, for example, the barring gene, the male has a double dose and the female a single dose leading to the male chicks having a lighter patch on the top of the head. This is more obvious if a barred cock is put onto a brown hen: the female chicks (single dose) have a small light spot on the head and on the males (double dose) it spreads over the body. The autosexing breeds have been produced to take advantage of this.

Male

Both right and left testes are located between the lungs and the kidneys, close under the spine. It is one of life's great unanswered questions how avian sperm survives normal avian body temperature (40-42° C, 104-108° F) when mammalian sperm must be stored outside the body at a degree or two lower in temperature in order to be viable. It may have something to do with the fact that sperm production time is much shorter

The two breeds which created the original sex-linked plumage, Rhode Island Red and Light Sussex, but it has to be a male RIR and a female LS in order to get the crossing over of the colours in the chicks with males yellow/white and females brown.

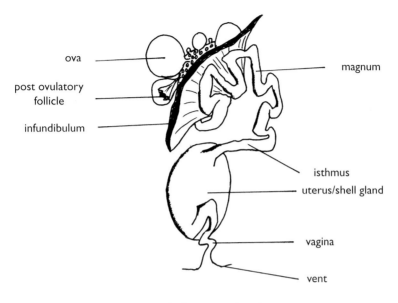

ova

post ovulatory
follicle

infundibulum

magnum

isthmus

uterus/shell gland

vagina

vent

Left ovary and oviduct

in birds than the 8 weeks in mammals but any stress will therefore affect sperm quality faster. The testes are at their largest in the breeding season and the volume of ejaculate is from 0.5ml-1.0ml. The avian sperm is thin (one third longer than in man) and is stored in host glands in the vagina. The turkey holds the viability record of 72 days, but normally this is 14 days in hens and 7 days in ducks, so if males need to be changed, wait the appropriate time to ensure the correct sire.

Waterfowl have a true phallus, whereas chickens, turkeys, pheasants, guinea fowl and quail have a small non-protruding phallus on the ventral lip of the vent which forms into a groove to pass semen to the female oviduct. This makes it easy to vent sex waterfowl when they are up to one month old (immature phallus) and after six months (mature phallus) and almost impossible to vent sex poultry at any age, unless training of five years has been undertaken.

Broilers have a fast feathering gene added so that wing feathers are longer in the female at hatch, but broiler breeders are vent sexed by trained operators. Some of these operators advertise that they can sex pure breeds, but the accuracy is only about 80% which can be achieved in some breeds by down colour in any case. For sexing methods, see Chapter 1, page 16 Caponisation (neutering) used to be practised by the insertion of an oestrogen capsule just behind the comb of males at 8 weeks, leaving an interval of at least 6 weeks until slaughter to avoid contamination of the meat. This is now illegal in the EU. Surgical castration of cockerels is also illegal in the UK.

Female

Only the left ovary and duct are normally functional in poultry. The number of possible eggs produced is genetically determined and fairly strongly inherited, hence the development of chickens specifically for laying. Chickens tend not to lay at the same time each day as they take about 25 hours to lay an egg. After ovulation the yolk leaves the ovary and enters the infundibulum (length 4", 10cm) for 15 minutes where fertilisation takes place and the chalazae (see below) are added. When the hen ovulates, sperm travels up from the vaginal storage glands to the infundibulum, ready to fertilise the egg. Next is the magnum (length 13", 33cm) where secretion and addition of albumen occurs during the following 3 hours. It is in the isthmus (length 4", 10cm) where the shell membrane is added, time here being $1\frac{1}{2}$ hours and then the major time component is in the uterus (length 4", 10cm) where the shell itself is laid down including any pigment, taking 20 hours. The egg only spends one minute in the 3" (8cm) long vagina before being laid. The oviduct is extruded through the cloaca so that although egg and faeces theoretically share the same exit, the egg is protected. Any dirt on the egg will be added in the nest from dirty feet. Thus a hen can only lay one egg per 24 hours and sometimes misses a day if at the time to ovulate it is dark as she normally ovulates $\frac{1}{2}$ an hour after laying.

A hen will lay every day and then miss a day; the number of eggs is called a clutch. The hen will go broody and incubate the eggs when she

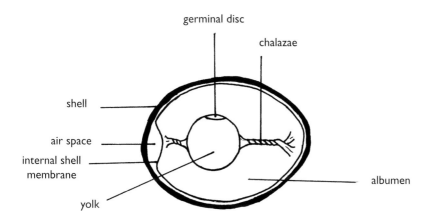

germinal disc

chalazae

shell

air space

internal shell
membrane

yolk

albumen

Diagrammatic contents of an egg

has laid a clutch or if there are many eggs in the nest. If the eggs are continually removed, she will lay for longer. If left in the nestboxes by mistake, lots of hens will go broody and then have to be broken off by using the sinbin - a cage with wire floor plus food and water for 14 days.

To test if a bird is in lay, put your fingers vertically between the pin bones - three fingers' width means she is laying and her vent will be moist and loose. Two or less fingers' width means she is not at present laying.

Ducks have the same system of laying eggs, but it happens in 24 hours, so they tend to lay at the same time each day, usually early in the morning - useful so they can be let out after laying as crows and magpies soon take the eggs otherwise.

Geese are usually happier laying every other day until their clutch is complete which they know by the feel of the amount of eggs in the nest. So if you remove their eggs, you can keep both ducks and geese laying longer than they would in the wild. Light breed hens and ducks come into lay at about 18-20 weeks old with heavy breed hens and ducks at 26+ weeks. Point-of-lay (POL) is the age of 18 weeks, when pullets are traditionally moved to laying quarters. It does not mean that the birds will lay the next day, but it is still used in advertisements. Young geese tend not to lay until the following spring, although older light breeds such as Chinese may lay in the autumn, but these eggs are less likely to be fertile.

Turkeys and guinea fowl either lay at 26+ weeks or wait until the following spring.

Pheasants lay at 1, 2 or more years old, depending on species, and seem to prefer the evening.

Quail are the fastest to mature, laying eggs at 6 weeks old, but their life expectancy is only 18 months.

For lighting regimes, see page 86. As mentioned in Chapter 4, the liver synthesises yolk protein and lipid and these are carried to the ovary in the bloodstream. The yolk is the main source of nutrient for the embryo and together with the germinal disc is known as the ova which is supported in the white by the chalazae. These are twisted strands of thick albumen which keep the yolk more or less central in the egg and ensure that the germinal disc is always on the top surface. The colour of the yolk depends on the amount of carotenoids the bird has eaten. These are contained in green plants, so outdoor birds on grass and herbs usually have dark yolks. Nearly all commercial feed contains yolk colorant (canthaxanthin is a favourite), but the better feed firms are at last realising that outdoor birds do not need it. The outer surface of the shell in most poultry is smooth with a slight sheen. Breeds laying highly pigmented eggs such as Welsummer or Maran add the pigment (certain individuals including spots and speckles) on top of the shell, so it can rub off. The Araucana is unique in that the blue/green pigment is throughout the shell. Duck eggs are slightly greasy and geese eggs are chalky. Pheasant eggs vary according to species with some shells so dense and dark that they are difficult to candle. Turkey eggs are almost invariably cream with brown speckles. Guinea fowl eggs are pale brown with speckles and have a very hard shell, but they do originate from a tropical climate so this may be to slow down evaporation. Quail eggs are heavily blotched with dark brown.

Incubation times

chickens	21 days	pheasants	24-28 days
ducks	28 days	turkeys	28 days
muscovies	35 days	guinea fowl	28 days
ornamentals	24-30 days	quail	17 days
geese	28-32 days		

White shelled eggs are the easiest to candle (look into with a bright torch to see the developing embryo) but even dark shelled eggs can be candled at 14 days of incubation with a fertile egg having a definite clear air space and dark embryo.

Incubated eggs should be transferred to the hatcher 2 days before they are due to hatch. The embryo penetrates the air space and breathes, then pips (a small triangular piece of shell is raised), using its egg tooth which falls off shortly after hatching. The chick rotates in the shell,

Examples of mis-shapen and slab-sided eggs, with a soft shelled egg. These may be due to IB or some other infection in the shell gland. The occasional strangely shaped or shell-less egg may just be due to the beginning or end of lay.

breaking it in a circle. Humidity should be high in the hatcher as the chick needs to break through not only the shell but the shell membrane which can dry out like leather and imprison it. The time to hatching from pipping is about 20 hours. Try to resist the temptation to help out chicks partly hatched after the main hatch has finished as they are likely to be poor doers. If there has been a problem during incubation, such as a power cut, or the broody hen leaving the nest, they may take longer to hatch anyway.

Take small pieces of shell off at a time with tweezers and if the membrane bleeds, stop, try again 4 hours later. Only if the membrane does not bleed can you take the broad end of the shell off as by this time the yolk should have been absorbed into the navel.

Egg quality is judged on internal contents and external appearance, whether for exhibition or consumption. A fresh egg has a raised yolk, thick albumen with a small airspace. A stale egg has a flat yolk, thin albumen and a large airspace. The shell should be smooth and regular and the shape should be an elliptical cone. Eggs for hatching should be collected regularly, washed in Virkon (water warmer than eggs so bacteria are not drawn into the eggs), stored in trays, sharp end down, at a temperature of 10°C (50°F). If they must be kept longer than a week then turn them by placing another tray on top and carefully inverting the trays once a day, but hatchability falls off dramatically after 7 days of even the best storage.

Problems/diseases

Egg eating: A difficult vice to cure, caused originally by poorly designed nestboxes, boredom, poor nutrition, a soft shelled egg laid on the floor or a broken egg. It takes very little time for the vice to spread. Eggs are, after all, an excellent source of nutrition. If noticed early on by perhaps a drop in expected egg numbers, small bits of shell on the ground or egg on the face of the culprit, an egg may be filled with strong curry and mustard and placed in the hut. If this does not work, scatter 10-15 pingpong or golf balls in the hut and remember to collect the eggs several times a day.

82

Egg peritonitis: Sometimes known as internal laying, the yolk misses the funnel of the infundibulum and descends into the abdominal cavity, particularly if the bird is stressed at ovulation. Mostly the yolk will be scavenged by the body defences, but occasionally several may descend together or infection sets in and the resulting peritonitis can quickly become fatal. The bird will be lethargic and depressed. There is no treatment.

Double yolks: Only a problem if the eggs are for hatching as no double yolker has been known to hatch and survive. This usually occurs in older hens and can come and go in various individuals.

Downgraded eggs: Occasionally meat or blood spots appear in eggs. These are harmless, but if eggs are sold they will be downgraded as it is an aesthetic problem. Sellers of eggs should remember that a cockerel should not be running with the hens, to avoid embryo development in poor storage conditions.

Hens that consistently lay eggs with slab-sided or wrinkled shells are likely to be carriers of infectious bronchitis (see page 71) and should be culled. Stress can result in the occasional odd-shaped egg, especially those with an equatorial bulge which results from rough handling of the bird. Hens which consistently lay thin, porous or soft shelled eggs may be suffering from a calcium imbalance(see below), poor nutrition, infectious bronchitis, excessive temperature, antimicrobials.

At the beginning and end of lay odd anomalous shaped eggs may appear. Loss of colour can indicate infectious bronchitis, although the very dark brown eggs will tend to fade as the hens reach the end of lay. Small eggs indicate either pullets just coming into lay or inadequate water or infectious bronchitis. IB is also indicated if the chalazae are ruptured.

Egg bound: Bird will stand hunched up. Usually due to a calcium imbalance which may be dietary or brought on by stress such as exhibiting. The bird needs to be kept warm as this is a sort of cramp and a little warm olive oil put into the vent. If the egg is partially out of the vent but still within the oviduct, it may be necessary to cut the membrane, but this may cause future egg laying problems. Calcium supplements will only be helpful if they are in a soluble and absorbable state. The Birdcare Company manufactures one called Calcivet, but it should only be used occasionally as if used all the time, the calcium regulatory mechanism becomes lazy.

Poor hatchability: Can be nutritional (see page 60), IB or other infection, poor egg storage, poor incubation technique. Or your breed of chicken may only hatch 50%; cross breeds can hatch 100%.

Infertility: This can be due to lack of sperm, lack of viable sperm, lack of energy or physical access being denied. Causes can include inbreeding, stress or certain antimicrobials. Some breeds have such fluffy feathers that the cocks cannot physically reach the hens and both sexes need feathers trimming or removing around the vents. Vent feathers clagged up with muck or lots of lice eggs on vent feathers will prevent access by the cockerel.

Heavy louse infestations may pull down the cockerel and any concurrent disease can make him infertile. If there is more than one cockerel they may be jealous of each other and push each other off the hens. Waterfowl may have had a prolapsed phallus which has subsequently got frostbite or gangrene and dropped off. It is worth checking (see sexing methods page 16)

Vent gleet: See page 29.

Prolapsed oviduct: The only sign may be a dead hen with her back end pecked out as hens are obsessively attracted to red and thus become cannibals. Stress, age, obesity and poor nutrition will all contribute to the condition.

Preferential mating: Bare necks, torn backs and loss of feathers denote a favourite female. Separate the cockerel or drake, stitch any fresh wounds and leave the hen or duck to heal in peace.

Salmonella pullorum: This can cause lesions in the ovary affecting egg production (see page 56).

Diseases passed through the egg

Viruses:

adenoviruses - quail bronchitis, haemorrhagic enteritis of turkeys, marble spleen disease of pheasants

reoviruses - viral arthritis

retroviruses - lymphoid leukosis

enteroviruses - duck viral hepatitis

Bacteria: salmonella, *E. coli,* staphylococci, mycoplasmas

Fungi: aspergillus

7 ENDOCRINE AND LYMPHATIC SYSTEMS

Endocrine

The pineal gland is the main one that concerns poultry keepers as this is the one supposedly controlling breeding hormones. It does this as it is affected by light levels and is stimulated by shortening day length followed by lengthening day length and provides control of egg production and spermatogenesis. Lighting programmes for winter laying need to commence after the days have got shorter, so early November is early enough to add light. The optimum length of daylight is 14 hours - more than this is merely a waste of electricity. It is important to have light bulbs of sufficient wattage: one 40W bulb would be suitable in a 6 sq ft hut. It should be bright enough to read the newspaper by. When lighting is started up, increase the hours gradually over two weeks until the magic 14 is reached. As hens like to go to bed before twilight it is best to have all the extra hours in the early morning, set on a timer. Alternatively use a dimmer for 15 minutes in the evening otherwise they will be stranded without finding a roost. Try not to alter the hours drastically once they have been reached as it can put the birds off lay, so keep a check that the light bulbs are all working.

Early breeding of heavy breeds is one way to maintain size so light can be gradually increased from the middle of November and if all goes well they should be laying by Christmas. Some of the heavy breeds refuse to be pushed, however, so don't be too disappointed if the older birds use the extra light as an excuse to eat more and get fat. Silkies have a penchant for laying and going broody in January with no extra light, and then of course are not broody when you want them to be in the spring.

Chicks which are brooded under infra-red lamps can suffer from excess light. The best infra-red bulbs are those with no light (dull emitters) and this means that chicks have to sleep at night and therefore grow both in body and in feather. If they have 24 hours' light they are prone to feather peck and will not grow as fast. Alternatively use an 'electric hen' type brooder which is a rectangular box on adjustable legs with a soft undercover and a heating element within. The chicks can press up to the heat just like a mother hen or go to a cooler area.

Lymphatic: The lymphatic vessels return fluids to the blood, keeping the general circulating volume of blood correct. Bone marrow, amongst other functions, is the source of stem cells ('grandparent' cells) which differentiate into the various leucocytes then lymphocytes which end up in the lymphoid tissue. The lymphoid tissue is responsible for adaptive immunity which is the response to specific antigens (the part of a pathogen that stimulates an immune response) and the conferring of resistance to subsequent infections. In mammals lymphoid tissue is contained in lymph glands, but the bird as usual is different. It has lymphoid tissue spread throughout all tissues of the body. There are also tonsils in the pharynx, at the junction of each caecum and smaller nodules throughout the digestive tract.

Ducks and geese have two pairs of true lymph nodes as well, but these are thought to be less efficient than mammals'. Birds have a thymus which tends to shrink as the bird reaches maturity (like mammals) and this is where the T cells (T lymphocytes) mature, then going on to populate the lymphoid tissue. The T cells are vital in maintaining the body's defence against pathogens.

Birds are unique in having a cloacal bursa, also known as the bursa of Fabricius. This, like the thymus, shrinks as the bird matures, but it produces B lymphocytes which migrate to the lymphoid tissue and produce antibodies and immunoglobulins in response to pathogens. The B cells and the T cells work together, conferring resistance and keeping the bird healthy. It is a delicate balance and if upset by stress (which produces immunosuppressive cortisol) the cells do not work as well, immunity is suppressed and the bird gets a disease. The spleen in birds is involved in the recycling of red blood cells and lymphocyte and antibody production, but it is not a reservoir of blood, as in mammals.

The young chicken is obviously sick: standing hunched with its tail and head down. This could be the early stages of coccidiosis, Gumboro (IBD) or Salmonellosis.

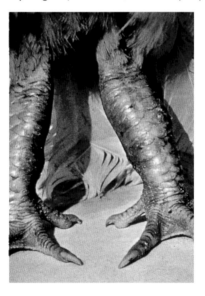

Osteopetrosis - 'thick leg disease' - uncommon in extensive flocks.

Problems/diseases

Leucosis/sarcoma group: This disease needs to be distinguished from Marek's, page 95. It may be a function of the lymphoid tissue distribution in birds, but tumours are common. Lymphoid leucosis is the most common of this group and is caused by a retrovirus. The lymphoid leucosis virus is a slowly transforming virus, taking about four months to kill a bird. Signs are weakness and emaciation with pale wattles, a swollen liver and possible diarrhoea. Paralysis is not a feature. Osteopetrosis (thickening of the long bones) is apparent - the disease used to be known as 'thick leg disease'. There may be tumours anywhere in the body. The disease is transmitted both vertically (through the egg) and horizontally (between birds). Some chicks born with the virus will tolerate it and live, but spend their lives shedding the virus into their eggs. The survival of the virus outside the body is only a few hours, so even though it is shed in saliva, faeces and feather debris, it is not very contagious. The virus is thought to be ubiquitous and many birds will have developed resistance. No treatment or vaccines are available, but some pure breeds are genetically resistant such as the Fayoumi.

Gumboro (Infectious Bursal Disease, IBD): The odd name was taken from where the disease was originally found in the USA. It mostly affects chickens from 3-6 weeks old and is a virus which attacks the bursa of Fabricius. It has a sudden onset, a short course of about a week and extensive destruction of lymphocytes, thereby leaving the bird, if it lives, open to any infection. Birds die within 2 days of the first signs (depression, off food and hunched up). The disease is highly infectious and contagious and survivors excrete the virus for 2 weeks. With antibiotic cover and lots of TLC, deaths can be kept to a minimum. There is a vaccine which seems to work well especially if given to breeding hens so that maternal antibody (passive immunity) is passed to the chick and it is then protected for about 4 weeks. This disease began in commercial flocks, but backyard flocks are vulnerable as the virus remains in the environment for 4 months.

8 CARDIOVASCULAR SYSTEM

The avian heart is large compared to that of mammals, probably developed in response to the tremendous demands of flying. The high cardiac output means that blood pressure is also high, but oxygen transport is very efficient. The heart is surrounded by the liver (as opposed to the lungs in mammals) and the right jugular vein is larger than the left. Blood sampling can be taken from the right jugular vein or the ulnar vein on the inside of the elbow. Bird red blood cells are nucleated which distinguishes them from mammalian blood cells, and they have heterophils instead of neutrophils (white blood cells). One per cent of total mass (10ml/kg) of blood can be collected from a healthy bird, less if the bird is sick. The agglutination blood test for BWD/fowl typhoid needs just a drop of blood, usually taken from the ulnar vein. The carotid arteries run in a ventral groove in the neck vertebrae and are covered by the neck muscles. They will still function if the throat of the bird is cut, therefore it is not a humane way to cull. Dislocation of the neck, as it severs the arteries, is the recommended humane way.

Birds have a renal portal shunt which means that blood can be diverted from or to the kidneys. This may help in increasing blood flow to the legs to assist with running. They keep their feet warm not only by sitting or perching on them and surrounding them with insulating feathers, but by a countercurrent system in the legs: the venous blood is warmed by the arterial blood and the blood flow is increased in cold weather. This is especially useful in waterfowl and enables them to roost and walk on ice without getting frostbite. The other heat exchanger in birds is in the head: arterial and venous blood is enmeshed and cooled with cooler venous blood from the nasal region.

There is an artery in the spur of cockerels, so cautery is needed if de-spurring or if a spur is broken.

Problems/diseases

Heart attack: Heavy breeds are prone to this, especially the one you are washing for a major show. An intermittent purple comb is indicative of heart disease which may be congenital. Turkeys have even higher blood pressure than other birds and can have a heart attack if badly stressed. High blood pressure is why birds bruise so easily.

Sodium toxicity: If chicks have an excess of salt in their diet this can result in heart damage and ultimately death.

Vitamin E deficiency: Lesions in the cardiac muscle responsive to vitamin E in ducks and turkeys are associated with excess heavy metals.

Furazolidone: Now banned from use in food producing species, this broad spectrum bactericidal drug causes cardiomyopathy (heart disease) in turkeys, less so in chickens and ducks.

Poisons: Phenols and coal tar products such as creosote damage blood vessels. See page 102.

Viral infection: Marek's disease (page 95) can produce lesions of the blood vessels or tumours in the heart.

Lymphoid leucosis causes tumours of the vascular system (haemangiosarcoma).

Bacterial infection: Erysipelas (see page 29) is implicated, as is BWD/fowl typhoid (see page 50), chlamydia (see page 74) and pasteurella (see page 73).

Atherosclerosis: As in humans, it is the overweight ones not taking any exercise that are liable to get furred up arteries. It is more prevalent in female birds due to the high levels of circulating fat needed for yolk formation. It is hereditary, but totally reversible by diet and exercise. Check the pelvic or pin bones to gauge fatness on poultry (see page 79)

Ascites: This is fluid in the abdomen. Bird has a floppy, distended abdomen. Broilers are prone to it because they grow very quickly and are prone to heart disease, which causes it. It is rare in outdoor birds which tend to be much slower growing, unless someone has mistakenly introduced broiler blood into a strain, thinking to increase size and growth.

Parasites: Avian blood parasites are rare, but global warming may encourage the vectors, mostly insects. Young birds are particularly at risk. **Injections:** If an injection is given in the leg of a bird, the renal portal shunt may not get the medicine to the correct place. It is safer to inject in the breast muscle (see page 19).

9 NERVOUS SYSTEM

Sensory and peripheral

The beak of poultry is sensitive, particularly so in ducks and geese. For filtering food they have special areas in the beak called Herbst corpuscles, plus a sensory bill tip organ, the nail. Beak trimming of chickens and turkeys to avoid cannibalism (and allow overcrowding) is no longer recommended on welfare grounds due to the pain. Herbst corpuscles are also throughout the skin of poultry, usually underneath the filamentous sensitive hairs. The chicken has 17 pairs of cervical nerves which form successive ring-like sensory cutaneous fields (this is is why a bird ruffles its feathers in sequence around its neck) along the neck and innervate feather follicles and smooth muscles which move the feathers. This system continues down the body.

The brachial plexus is more highly developed in the wings of flying birds and the lumbosacral plexus is more highly developed in terrestrial birds. Unlike mammals, the spinal nerves near the tail exit the vertebral canal at the synsacrum and at right angles to it. The lumbosacral plexus is embedded in the kidneys and can therefore be affected by an inflammatory kidney disease due to pressure. The main nerve supplying the legs is the ischiatic nerve which is the largest nerve in the avian body. The tail is well supplied with nerves: it needs to be a rudder when flying, and preening and other behavioural actions are important. The turkey or peacock would not be the same without its tail display. At day-old, nerves in the metacarpus are poorly developed, so pinioning of waterfowl is done at this time. Wing tags are placed in the propatagium (flap of skin between elbow and metacarpus) as this flap of skin is not well innervated.

Autonomic

The parasympathetic system conserves body reserves and the sympathetic system produces responses appropriate to fight or flight. Both have afferent (towards the CNS therefore sensory) and efferent (away from CNS therefore motor) fibres and cooperate to preserve homoeostasis of the internal environment, usually by means of a dual innervation for each organ. Birds have a similar system of reflex arcs to mammals.

Problems/diseases

Beak trimming: This causes a severe setback to the birds, even when done at the usual time of 10 days. Some commercial layer suppliers still do it: if you do not want it done, check before you buy.

Culling: Every bird twitches and flaps when culled, no matter what method has been used, so be prepared for movement. Traditionally, turkeys are slaughtered head down in a cone to prevent wing bruising and damage.

Hypermetria: a high-stepping gait due to a functional failure in the cerebellum (centre of motor activity in the brain, particularly concerned with movement). May be inherited, in which case no treatment.

Poisoning: Various poisons cause nervous signs including lead and zinc (see Poisons, page 100)

Botulism: The bacteria is *Clostridium botulinum* which produces an often fatal toxin, proliferating in hot weather when water levels are low and dirty. Carcases will produce maggots and only 3 or 4 of these, infected with botulism, can kill a duck. The signs are sudden death or flaccid paralysis with the neck not being supported. If the neck is floppy then antitoxin is required. Mild cases may recover with oral fluid therapy plus activated charcoal and bismuth.

Nutritional disorders: Thiamine deficiency will produce stargazing (head permanently tipped up towards the sky), vitamin A deficiency may produce weakness and paralysis of chicks and vitamin E deficiency may produce stargazing and muscular dystrophy, chicks dying at less than 3 weeks old (see page 60).

Other diseases: The following all have nervous signs associated with them and have been described elsewhere:
Duck viral enteritis (page 58),
Duck viral hepatitis (page 57),
Derzsy's disease (page 97),
Newcastle disease (page 97),
Pasteurella anatipestifer (page 73)

Hawaiian Geese (Nene): There is a hereditary disease of Nenes which is due to cerebral lipidosis and results in progressive hind limb weakness. Check breeding records to avoid this.

Marek's disease: First described in 1907 by the Hungarian veterinarian Josef Marek, it is caused by a herpes virus which prefers lymphoid tissue and causes tumours in the ovary, lung, heart, liver, kidney, spleen, skin, muscle: wherever lymphoid tissue is. Peripheral nerves are enlarged and classically the signs are paralysis with one wing and one leg forward and back. There may also be torticollis (twisting of the neck).

At post mortem the brachial and lumbosacral plexuses are enlarged. Birds from 6 weeks are affected, but it is most frequent between 12 and 24 weeks. Infection occurs by inhalation and following an acute phase four days later with few clinical signs, the infection becomes latent. The virus is spread throughout the body by infected lymphocytes and 2 weeks later infectious virus is shed into the environment in feather debris and dander (small scales from hair or feathers). The incubation period to clinical signs can range from 4 weeks to several months. The virus is ubiquitous throughout the world, but it is not transmitted through the egg and thus chicks are hatched free of infection. However, the virus is so infectious that they soon become infected. Once contracted, the infection persists throughout the life of the chicken, contaminating the environment by shedding the virus the while. The virus can survive in poultry house dust and litter for at least one year.

The genetic constitution of a chicken will influence its susceptibility to Marek's. Silkies and Sebrights are particularly prone, females more so than males. Fayoumis are resistant. The time of infection has a bearing on resistance - the older a chicken is before it meets the virus, the better able it is to resist it. Stress is the main environmental factor associated with increased incidence of the disease. Control is by vaccination which prevents the virus from being shed but does not necessarily prevent the disease. More virulent strains appear from time to time which means changing or improving the vaccine.

The classic pose of Marek's disease with one leg forward and one back and the wings either paralysed or being used for balance. Sometimes a bird may just be slightly lame.

10 OTHER (MISCELLANEOUS) DISEASES

Some of the following diseases are common and important, others are rare.

Viral

Paramyxovirus (Newcastle Disease or Fowl Pest): first isolated in 1926. All birds are susceptible especially chickens and turkeys. Signs are very variable and range from respiratory, nervous, a drop in egg production, soft shelled eggs, greenish loose faeces, torticollis (twisting of the neck) to sudden death. Pigeon paramyxovirus reached the UK in 1983 and has caused outbreaks in flocks through contamination of feed. Newcastle Disease is notifiable.

The virus survives in the dead host for several weeks at cool temperatures or several years if frozen, and in faeces for over a month. Birds imported into the UK from outside the EU have to be quarantined for 35 days and have 8 week old, unvaccinated chickens as sentinels (unvaccinated birds which are post mortemed at the end of quarantine to see if they have acquired ND from birds in quarantine) in order to prevent Newcastle disease from entering. The UK is mostly clear of it, but outbreaks do occur from time to time (the last one via wild waterfowl) and only in the face of an outbreak is vaccination recommended, but racing pigeons are compulsorily vaccinated.

ND is zoonotic with flu-like symptoms and conjunctivitis.

Parvovirus: Derzsy's disease or goose viral hepatitis affects goslings and muscovy ducklings at less than one month old. Birds will suffer from diarhhoea, leg weakness and swollen heads. There is a vaccination for breeding birds.

Pneumovirus: Turkey rhinotracheitis which affects intensively reared meat birds. Disease appears from 3-10 weeks of age and signs are mostly respiratory. There is a vaccine.

Adenoviruses: Quail bronchitis, turkey haemorrhagic enteritis (THE) and marble spleen disease in pheasants are caused by the same virus but have different effects. The signs in turkeys are sudden deaths over a 5-10 day period, bloodstained tail feathers and a pale carcase. In more chronic cases the birds are depressed and sit on their hocks with dark tarry droppings. There is no treatment, but chilling is thought to be a predisposing factor. Birds recover in about 2 weeks. The signs in pheasants include an enlarged and mottled spleen and death from asphyxia due to fluid on the lungs.

Egg drop syndrome '76: A natural virus of waterfowl which got into a chicken vaccine. It is really a problem of commercial layers as the signs are loss of shell strength and pigmentation, followed by thin shelled, soft shelled and shell-less eggs. Misshapen eggs are not a feature. There is a vaccine.

Bacterial

Mycobacterium avium **or avian tuberculosis (TB):** all poultry and waterfowl and most wild birds are susceptible to avian TB. It tends to be a disease of birds older than about 2 years. Stress can be a predisposing factor and the organism is slow growing, causing an insidious and chronic wasting disease with tuberculous lesions anywhere in the body. The appetite remains good while the bird loses weight and seems bright but weak. There is no treatment, although a vaccine is being trialled. Culling is best to remove one source of the bacteria. Valuable chicken flocks can be tested with a skin test, developed originally for cattle TB testing as a comparison with bovine TB. This is done into one wattle and if there is no swelling 48 hours later, the bird is pronounced clear.

Other

Clostridial diseases: Ulcerative enteritis (quail disease) usually affecting intensive flocks. Symptom is diarrhoea. Treatment is with penicillin or lincomycin.

Necrotic enteritis: Affects chickens and turkeys over 4 weeks. Coccidiosis (page 54) predisposes and turkeys develop a high pitched voice. Treatment is with penicillin or lincomycin.

Pasteurella-like organisms:

Yersinia pseudotuberculosis: There are tuberculous-like lesions in the lungs and liver, enlarged spleen and enteritis. Turkeys are most susceptible and signs include persistent diarrhoea, weakness, ruffled feathers, lameness and progressive emaciation. Rodents, especially mice, are carriers, so try and exclude these vermin.

Infectious coryza (*Haemophilus paragallinarum*): Not at present in UK. Signs are conjunctivitis, nasal discharge, facial and wattle swelling. Susceptible species are chickens, pheasants, quail and turkeys. There is a vaccine.

11 POISONS
AND TOXINS

Poultry are affected by many toxins and poisons. Prevention is the best course as there are few antidotes available. Keeping birds away from potential toxic materials is sensible, but better still not to use anything toxic in the garden, such as slug pellets.

Plants

Where plants are concerned, most poultry will not eat poisonous ones due to their bitter taste, but be especially careful of laburnum seeds, potato sprouts, black nightshade, henbane, most irises, privet, rhodedendron, oleander, yew, castor bean, sweet pea, rapeseed, corn cockle, clematis, common St John's Wort, meadow buttercup, vetch, ragwort and fungi (toadstools etc.). Blue-green algae is quickly fatal, so keep water containers clean, especially in hot weather and try and prevent access to stagnant water.

Toxic chemicals

Arsenic used in sprays for plants, rat and ant poisons and for tanalising timber, but this last is only a problem if the timber is still wet from the treatment. Clinical signs are nervous signs such as twitching and lack of co-ordination leading to death.

Copper: either as copper sulphate or copper oxychloride fungicides. Convulsions and death follow ingestion.

Calcium: excess due to supplementation will result in kidney failure. Young birds are more susceptible than adults.

Lead: from old paint, lead shot, fishermen's lead weights (both lead weights and lead shot are no longer used on waterways, but there is still bound to be a residue). Treatable if caught early enough by administration of sodium calciumedetate. Signs are green diarrhoea, muscle weakness and weight loss, confirmed by blood analysis. The head and neck may be swollen with a discharge from the eyes and nose.

Zinc: ingestion of galvanised wire, old galvanised drinkers. Signs are weight loss and leg weakness, confirmed by blood analysis. Treat as for lead poisoning.

Mercury: these compounds are used for treating grain and are cumulative. Signs are weight loss and leg weakness. Residues may be present in eggs and meat for several months after exposure to the poison.

Phosphorus: found in rodent baits, matches and fireworks. Causes sudden death or progressive weakness.

Nitrates: nitrate fertilisers cause increased thirst, purple comb in chickens, convulsions and death. Intravenous administration of methylene blue is the antidote.

Phosphides: found in rodent baits. Causes reduced appetite, coma and death.

Bicarbonates: young chicks and turkey poults are susceptible and the signs are diarrhoea, increased water consumption, death.

Sodium chloride common salt causes poisoning in excess. Road salt can be a problem in some areas where water courses are affected. Kidney failure, convulsions and death are the result.

Potassium permanganate was used as a disinfectant for incubators and causes sudden death if ingested.

Fungicides: these are used as seed protectants and produce depressed growth and deformities in young birds, with layers producing odd shaped, thin shelled, infertile eggs.

Herbicides any organophosphorus ingredient is dangerous. Paraquat produces convulsions and death with geese regurgitating crop contents.

Insecticides: chlorinated hydrocarbons: aldrin (grain treatment), chlordane, dieldrin (seed and timber protectant), DDT, lindane (only recently banned from louse powder). All of these can cause hyperexcitability followed by death. Be especially careful of woodshavings from treated wood. Shavings sold for livestock are from untreated wood.

Organophosphorus compounds: diazinon, dichlorvos, malathion, parathion, dimethoate. These are cumulative and result in regurgitation, muscle twitching and death. Can be one to three weeks before effect. Carbamates can kill chicks, poults and ducklings quickly.

Molluscicides: metaldehyde slug bait kills poultry. Good slug control in the garden is achieved by letting a few call ducks free range. They are small enough not to do damage to plants.

Rodenticides: surprisingly, chickens are relatively resistant to warfarin, but those baits based on phosphorus, arsenic or zinc phosphide are very toxic to poultry.

Phenolic compounds: many disinfectants are based on these, plus wood preservatives, coal tar products and creosote. This last kills young poultry and pheasants unless allowed to dry for at least three weeks before putting birds in a treated area. Traditionally used to kill red mite in henhouses, but there are now other products more effective and less toxic to the birds. Rinse any drinkers or feeders well if phenolic disinfectants have been used.

Formaldehyde causes conjunctivitis and respiratory distress.

Drugs: too high a dose or prolonged treatment or mixing incompatible ones will cause problems. Always follow veterinary advice. Ivomec is a useful parasiticide but is not licensed for poultry and in excess will make birds infertile or kill them. Ornamental geese seem more susceptible.

Ionophore coccidiostats (monensin, narasin and salinomycin) will kill turkeys and guinea fowl. Always read the label on feed bags.

Furazolidone, although now banned from food producing animals, kills chickens, turkeys and ducklings.

Sulphonamides are used to treat coccidiosis and can be toxic if the dose is exceeded or prolonged.

Mycotoxins: aflatoxin in feed eg. groundnuts, corn, cottonseed. Drought conditions for a crop encourages aflatoxins, but most reputable feed mills test for this.

Fusarium moulds occur on grains grown in cool climates.

Ergots are fungus on grass and grain flowering heads. Prevent the above by obtaining feed from a reputable source and store dry.

Other toxins: *E. coli* produces bacterial endotoxins which cause intoxication.

Renal or hepatic disease is caused when toxic products accumulate.

Clostridium botulinum **toxin** (see page 94).

Carbon monoxide: associated with the burning of fuel in an inadequate supply of oxygen. Chick gas heaters need ventilation, regular servicing and checking. The blood of dead chicks is bright cherry red.

Ammonia in concentrations of 170ppm causes conjunctivitis, paralysis of the tracheal cilia (see Respiratory chapter, page 67) and predisposes to more severe respiratory disease caused by a variety of respiratory pathogens. Keep litter dry and friable to avoid build up of ammonia and sufficient ventilation. If you can smell ammonia it will be adversely affecting the birds.

12 HOMEOPATHY

The word is derived from the Greek and means treating like with like. It is safe, gentle and effective and well worth a try. It is essentially a natural healing process, providing remedies to assist the patient to regain health by stimulating the body's natural forces of recovery. It concentrates on treating the patient, rather than the disease. Samual Hahnemann refined the principles, known since Hippocrates (450 BC), and proved them on himself. He discovered that a medicine which in large doses produces the symptoms of a disease will in small doses cure that disease and by extreme dilution, the medicine's curative properties are enhanced and all the poisonous side effects are lost. Homeopathic medicines are made in various potencies, but the 6C strength is recommended for poultry and as the tablets are small, they are easily put down the throat of a bird. The most useful remedies I have found are

Sulphur and **Silicea** for bumblefoot

Arnica for wounds and

Aconite for early infections.

Silicea is useful following egg binding as it helps to break down scar tissue.

Bryonia is useful for old geese with arthritis.

Gelsemium helps to calm show birds and

Euphrasia helps conjunctivitis.

Homeopathic remedies are worth experimenting with. They can sometimes be more effective than drugs, but I am not convinced that nosodes, the homeopathic form of vaccination, are as successful.

13 BASIC POULTRY
DISEASES CHART

This is an attempt to summarise the common poultry diseases found in small flocks. It is essential to involve your veterinary surgeon if you have problems with your poultry and although some wormers and louse powder can be obtained through licensed outlets, most drugs and medicines are only obtainable through a vet. Wash hands after handling medicines and observe the withdrawal instructions on the labels of drugs, so do not eat eggs or birds when medicines are being given. If medicines are given in water, make no other water is available. Most diseases are management related, for instance rats and mice carry some diseases as well as all those carried by wild birds, so many diseases can be prevented by good management.

Some species are susceptible to certain drugs, particularly guinea fowl, so care is needed with administration. Some poultry diseases are zoonotic (transmissable to humans), so personal hygiene care is needed with sick birds. There are other diseases found such as cancer, but most poultry will be healthy if they are fed on high quality feed, kept in relatively stress-free conditions, rat and mouse free with plenty of fresh air.

COMMON PROBLEMS AND SOME CAUSES

Weight loss: liver disease, starvation, bullying, avian TB, Northern fowl mite or red mite, poisoning, coccidiosis, kidney disease, lack of water, high levels of ammonia.

Diarrhoea: *E. coli,* BWD, coccidia, too much cabbage, hexamita, *Salmonella typhimurium* or *enteritidis,* sudden change of diet. Do not confuse caecal contents with diarrhoea.

Missing feathers: moulting, pushing head through fence, hens plucking each other or the cock (culprit usually has all feathers), claws of male, poor nutrition.

No eggs: birds too young, days too short, IB, fright/stress, new home, rats or magpies stealing eggs, birds laying away, laid on floor and buried, eaten by hens, not enough food, too much food, northern fowl mite or red mite.

Chick discomfort: noisy when defecating and pasted up vent= *E. coli,* continual cheeping = too cold, hungry, thirsty, one escaped from brooder, panting = too hot, huddled together = too cold.

Respiratory noises: mycoplasmosis, IB, aspergillosis, high levels of ammonia, gapeworm.

EGGS:

Infertile: excess males, flea eggs on vent, too many feathers on vent, cock too old.

Not hatching: not know correct incubation time, not fertile, infected by hen.

Dead in shell: dirty shell/nest, 'banger' (egg exploded in incubator because rotten), too much humidity in setter, not enough humidity in hatcher, sat on by broody before collection, poor nutrition of breeders, poor egg storage, eggs too old, old age of hen, drugs at incorrect levels, *Salmonella pullorum* infection, damaged shell, malposition (head in small end).

CHICKS:

Early hatch: very small bantams, eggs too fresh, sat on by broody before collection.

Unhealed navel: eggs too old, temperature of incubator too low, too much humidity in setter.

Deformities: genetic or nutritional, slippery surface for first few days.

Deaths: Salmonella, coccidiosis, chilling, smothering.

Sudden death in adults: egg peritonitis, heart attack, Gumboro, Salmonella, stoat/mink/ferret, choked, kidney failure, aspergillosis, botulism

COMMON DISEASES BY AGE

Chicks: deformities (bent toes, crossed beak, splay leg), *E. coli*, BWD, Gumboro, IB, coccidiosis, starve outs, feather pecking, *Salmonella pullorum*. Natural rearing: the above plus chilling, squashed, vermin.

Growers (8-26 weeks): northern fowl mite/red mite, scaly leg, coccidiosis, rattly breathing (mycoplasmosis), swollen sinus, feather pecking, angel wing, perosis, smothering, Marek's, lameness (waterfowl worms), roach back, wry tail, cow hocks, impacted gizzard, roundworms, breathing difficulty (IB), poisoning, blackhead, aspergillosis, lice.

Adults & aged: egg peritonitis, avian TB, heart attack, scaly leg, northern fowl mite/red mite lice, rattly breathing (mycoplasmosis), swollen sinus, ear canal infection, bumblefoot, vent gleet, wet feather, arthritis, choking, sour crop, impacted crop, impacted gizzard, tumours, poisoning, aspergillosis.

Symptoms	Disease	Cause
Listless, head sunk into neck, white diarrhoea, maybe blood in droppings	Coccidiosis	Coccidia parasite
Listless, head sunk into neck, yellow diarrhoea	Blackhead	Parasite carried by heterakis worm
White diarrhoea, thirst, sudden death	Bacilliary White Diarrhoea (BWD)	*Salmonella pullorum* bacteria
Listless, greenish diarrhoea, gaping, waterfowl off legs	Worms	Up to 6 different species of worm in different internal parts
Visible parasites round vent, listless, small blood spots on egg shells, whitish powder around perches	Lice or mites	4 types of louse, 2 types of mite
Sneezing, discharge from nostrils, foam in corner of eye. Rattly breathing. Swollen sinus under eye. Sweet sickly smell.	Mycoplasma (roup).	Bacteria
Swollen sinus in ducks.	Mycoplasma or Pseudomonas	Bacteria
Raised, encrusted scales on legs	Scaly leg	Mite, burrowing under s
Blood	Wounds	Feather-pecking due to h stress or overcrowding. Accidental cut. Fighting.

Treatment	Bird species
Coxi Plus or Proleth (not licensed for poultry) in water for 5 days. Coxoid.	All birds from 3 weeks
Emtryl in water for 5 days	Turkeys, pheasants, guinea fowl, rare in fowl but if fowl wormed, heterakis vector removed
Blood test to find and cull carriers	Chicks 0-3 weeks, adults as carriers
Flubenvet mixed into feed in trough for 7 days, 1 tablespoon to 4lb feed. Ivomec (not licensed for poultry) 5 drops on bird skin.	Fowl, ducks, geese, turkeys, pheasants, guinea fowl, peafowl, quail
Dust with pyrethrum based louse powder all over bird, spray housing crevices and perches for red mite with Duramitex. Remove eggs on base of feathers. Or Ivomec 5 drops on bird skin.	All poultry (wild birds carry mites)
Control by injecting Tylan 200 0.5ml per adult in breast muscle, 1ml for turkeys. Repeat after 48 hours. Mild cases Tylan soluble in water.	Fowl, turkeys, peafowl, pheasants, ducks.
Lance and flush with Baytril 2.5%. 5ml teal, 30ml swan daily for 5 days	Waterfowl
Dunk legs in surgical spirit once a week for three weeks. Do not pull off crusts. Takes a year to look normal. (Or use Ivomec 5 drops on bird skin.)	Any bird
Remobe the red colour, spray with coloured antiseptic, put Stockholm Tar on area. Isolate until healed.	Young stock or any bird.

Symptoms	Disease	Cause
Brown diarrohea, slow growth, sickly smell, poor feathering	Enteritis	*Escherichia coli (E. coli)* bacteria, stress, dirty conditions
Noxious smell, scabby vent	Vent gleet	Herpes virus
Purple comb when normally bright red	Heart disease, nitrate poisoning	Age, disease or deformity
Round swelling on underside of foot	Bumble foot	Staphylococcus bacteria entry due injury
Top beak overgrown, long claws	Overgrowth	Slight deformity of beak not symmetrical, ground too soft to wear claws
Sides of females bare of feathers or bleeding	Bareback	Sharp claws or spurs of males
Unusual behaviour	Stress	Disturbance or major changes
Lameness (if waterfowl see 'worms')	Injury or internal problem	Possibly a tumour
Wasting away but still feeding and alert	Avian tuberculosis	Bacteria
Paralysis, sometimes same side leg and wing	Marek's disease	Herpes virus

Treatment	Bird species
Terramycin in the water or Apralan or Baytril if bacteria immune.	Young stock of all poultry from 5 days
Topical antibiotics may help but culling advised.	Birds over 1 year
No treatment if heart, methylene blue if nitrate poisoning	Fowl
Very difficult to cure due to location. Some success with sulphur/silicea tablets or longterm antibiotic cover.	Old heavy birds, perches too high, any bird
Trim with dog nail clippers, careful not to cut the quick, cauterise with styptic pencil if bleeding occurs	All birds
Cut or trim spurs with hacksaw, careful of quick, file smooth and rounded.	All male birds
Vitamin powder in water or feed. Probiotic powder in water or feed.	Any bird. Stress can depress immune system causing dormant illness to flourish
Keep quiet and isolated. If an injury it should heal. If a tumour it will get worse. No treatment.	Any bird
No treatment - carried by wild birds. Natural immunity possible.	Birds over 1 year
Vaccination possible but not always effective. Cull affected birds.	Hens coming up to point of lay. Young cockerels

Symptoms	Disease	Cause
Some respiratory distress, loss of egg quality	Infectious bronchitis	Virus
Light weight, lethargic	Weight loss	Lack of feed, poor feed, bullying, internal parasites
Respiratory distress, gasping	Aspergillosis	Fungus
Pendulous crop	Cropbound	Old fibrous grass, poor muscle tone
Sudden chick deaths followed by recovery in rest of flock	Gumboro (Infectious Bursal Disease, IBD)	Virus
Cheesey substance in ear canal	Ear infection	Bacteria
Cheesey substance in mouth and throat	Oral canker (Trichomoniasis)	Protozoan
Listless, straining	Egg binding	A form of cramp
Wing droops then sticks out on young waterfowl	Angel wing	Too much protein
Waterfowl no longer waterproof	Wet feather	Shaft lice, excessive preening, mould

Treatment	Bird species
Vaccination effective	Fowl, pheasants, guinea fowl. Adults are carriers, 40% chick mortality
Give more feed/feeders, remove bully. Worm with Flubenvet	Any bird
Cull and remove infective hay or litter	0-4 weeks chicks, turkeys, waterfowl, pheasants
Isolate with just water for 48 hours. If not improved, massage crop contents out by holding bird upside down, giving it time to breathe. May need surgery to remove impaction	Old hens or birds on long grass or hay
Vaccination effective, antibiotic cover useful	1-16 weeks
Antibiotic ointment, some success with Leo Yellow mastitis tubes or dog ear drops (Surolan)	Any bird
Emtryl in water, but takes a long time to clear	Any bird
Keep bird warm until egg is passed, putting a little warm olive oil on vent. Give Calcivet or Nutrobal in water. Check diet, remove stressor	Any female bird
Tape wing in natural position for 3 days, do again if necessary. Reduce protein in feed (wheat)	Growing waterfowl
Keep off water, de-louse, if mould wash in detergent. Next moult feathers may be OK	Waterfowl

113

GLOSSARY

Agglutination blood test: a simple test for *Salmonella pullorum* or *S. gallinarum*. One drop of blood is placed on a plate and one drop of reagent added. If the blood clumps (agglutinates) then the test is positive and the bird should be culled.

Antibiotic: a chemical substance which either kills or inhibits growth of microorganisms.

Antimicrobial: a chemical substance which either kills or inhibits growth of microorganisms - a more general term than antibiotic.

AOC/AOV: Any Other Colour, Any Other Variety in show classes.

Ark: moveable triangular shaped house and run with mesh sides for poultry. Originally designed to stop sheep jumping on top.

Autosexing: created varieties of chickens which have different coloured or patterned down on the chicks according to their sex at day-old.

Aviary: a solid roofed pen for pheasants or other flying poultry with at least one wire mesh side, usually containing shrubs for food or cover and grass, sand or bark chips on the floor. Deep litter can be used with access to a grass run for hens.

Bactericidal: a chemical which kills bacteria.

Bacteriostatic: a chemical which inhibits the growth or multiplication of bacteria.

Bantam: a small breed of hen without a large counterpart. Miniature is one quarter the size of a large breed, but current usage of bantam encompasses both. True bantam is specific. See Appendix III.

Bit: a nearly circular piece of plastic temporarily inserted between the top and bottom mandible of hens with the ends lodged in the nostrils. Prevents feather pecking and cannibalism while allowing feeding and drinking to take place.

Bloom: the translucency of skin with a thin layer of fat under it of a turkey or chicken old enough to be ready for the table.

Bow-legged: greater distance between the legs at the hocks than at the feet.

Brood patch: the bare area of skin on the breast of a bird so that the eggs are kept moistened and warmed. The feathers grow back outside the breeding season.

Broody: the trance-like state of a hen when she is hormonally programmed to incubate eggs.

Bursa: small fluid filled sac in places where friction would otherwise occur. Bursa of Fabricius is involved in the immune system.

Caeca: the paired (single=caecum) blind-ended intestinal sacs where digestion of cellulose takes place by fermentation. The contents are voided at about every tenth dropping and the colour can vary depending on state of health or diet.

Candling: the process of looking into an egg by shining a narrow beam of light through the shell, preferably in a darkened room. This is to make sure of freshness by the size of the airspace, find any blood or meat spots, or to ascertain if the egg is fertile after about 7 days of incubation, when a spider shape of blood vessels can be seen if fertile. White shells are easiest to see through and dark brown or green ones the most difficult.

Caponisation: a chemical method of castrating male birds, now illegal.

Capture myopathy: stressed birds, particularly waterfowl, following catching and transport, may stay sitting down for a day or so. As long as they are able to reach feed and water, recovery is usually spontaneous.

Carotenoids: orange, red or yellow pigments found in green leaves and carrots. An artificial form is added to commercial feed so that the colour of yolks is darkened (canthaxanthin).

Carpus: the last joint of the wing to which the primary flight feathers are attached. This is the portion removed when waterfowl are pinioned at day-old.

Caruncles: fleshy protruberances on the face of male muscovies and male turkeys.

Cellulitis: painful swelling of tissues, usually just under the skin. The inflammatory process is caused by reaction to infection with bacteria, usually Streptococcus or Staphylococcus.

Chromosome: gene containing DNA and transmitting genetic material.

Cloaca: external opening equivalent to the anus in mammals.

Clutch: the number of eggs laid daily before a day is missed. Traditionally, an odd number of eggs which a broody hen can comfortably incubate (bantam 7, large fowl 13). An odd number fits neatly into a circle i.e. a nest.

Coccidia: a parasite colonising the intestinal tract of poultry, most types being **pathogenic** and causing enteritis.

Coccidiostats: drugs which control the multiplication of coccidia to below pathogenic levels, but with sufficient parasites remaining to produce an immunity.

Comb: fleshy protruberance, bright red in good health, on the head of poultry, usually larger in males. Types include single, rose, walnut, pea, cup, leaf, horn.

Commensal: an organism which normally lives on or in an animal without causing harm.

Coverts: small covering feathers on tail and wings.

Cow hocks: weakness at hocks, hocks close together instead of apart.

Countercurrent: flowing in opposite directions, so that arterial and venous blood can exchange heat through parallel vessels, keeping the brain cool and the feet warm.

Crop tube: a method of administering medicine by tube down the throat and into the crop.

Cull: the removal or killing of birds which are deformed, ill or surplus to a breeding programme.

Dead-in-shell: embryos in eggs which are due to hatch die a day or so beforehand. Causes of embryonic death include bacterial contamination, poor or prolonged storage before incubation, poor nutrition of parent stock, shell abnormalities or cracks, incubator faults.

Disinfectant: an agent which destroys infection-producing organisms. Try and use disinfectants approved for poultry use by MAFF as these will be the most effective and least toxic to the birds.

Down: the first fluffy covering of a day-old chick, duckling or gosling. Replaced by feathers at about six weeks. Also the warm underfeathering of waterfowl.

Downies: young waterfowl before they get their true feathers.

Drench: a method of administering medicine by tube down the throat.

Duck-footed: a deformity in chickens consisting of the rear toe lying close to the floor instead of spread out, thus resembling the foot of a duck.

Dwarfing gene: in Scots Dumpy and Japanese chickens, where the shank is very much reduced in length, the rest of the body being normal. When breeding, only 25% of the chicks have the requisite short legs.

ELISA test: enzyme-linked immunosorbent assay. A laboratory test using fresh blood, developed to measure exposure to a disease.

Emphysema: non painful, abnormal air in subcutaneous tissues.

Endotoxin: toxin produced by intestinal bacteria.

Enteritis: inflammation of the digestive tract usually resulting in diarrhoea.

Fleas: external parasites. Rare in fowl. Usually referring to **lice**.

Flea powder/louse powder: a topical external parasiticide, the most efficient chemical is **pyrethrum** based.

Fold unit: housing for poultry with a fixed run area, able to be moved on a regular basis over grass.

Foxproof enclosure: six foot high netting with a two foot overhang at the top and two foot of wire laid on the ground facing outwards and pegged is proven against foxes. Some people use electric netting at top and bottom of a six foot fence which works well as long as the current is present. Ornamental waterfowl are usually kept in this type of enclosure.

Free-range: the egg sales regulations state that free-range laying hens should have access to ground mostly covered by vegetation. Mud does not equal free-range and in severe weather, hens are best kept indoors, while waterfowl are fine as long as their water is accessible. Roaming at will may be a better definition.

Fret marks: these are horizontal marks on feathers denoting a nutritional stress when the feather was being formed. They should disappear at the next moult.

Galvanised drinker: useful until the galvanising starts to decay, when zinc poisoning may become a problem.

Grit: usually sold as mixed poultry grit, this is needed for the grinding of feed in the gizzard and the production of egg shells.

Gular flutter: the fluttering of the throat in warm weather in order to cool down.

Hay: never use as litter due to the moulds present.

Heterophil: avian equivalent of a **white blood cell** involved in disease control.

Hock: joint of the thigh with the **shank** of the leg (scaly part).

Homeostasis: being able to maintain a stable state in all body systems.

Housing: shelter and/or nesting areas for poultry.

Hyperthermia: increased body temperature. May be in response to an infection, or high external temperature. Sunstroke can happen, especially if water is limited.

Hypothermia: lowered body temperature. Hens are susceptible if they are wet and in a draught. Can kill if not noticed.

Imprinting: the instinctive attachment to a moving object which then becomes 'mother', most pronounced in downies. Males may not breed with their own species if imprinted.

Inbreeding: breeding between close relations: brother to sister, mother to son, father to daughter for instance. Grandparent to grandchild is all right.

Intersex: intermingling of both sex's characteristics (see Appendix III)

Knock-kneed: hocks close together instead of well apart.

Leucocytes/lymphocytes: white blood cells necessary for controlling disease.

Lice: feather lice are long and narrow bodied and are a nuisance, but not life-threatening.

Litter: any dry substance for the floor of a henhut or shelter, usually woodshavings or straw. Never use hay or any wet material.

MAFF: Ministry of Agriculture, Fisheries and Food. Address in phone book under Agriculture, Ministry of.

Mites: red mite and northern fowl mite are both bloodsuckers and can be life-threatening.

Mould: any mould is dangerous to poultry due to their intricate respiratory system. Keep all litter dry.

Notifiable: diseases which must be notified to MAFF if they are suspected, such as Newcastle disease, avian influenza.

Oestrogen: female sex hormone

Ova: female germ cells which can be subsequently fertilised for reproduction.

Ovary: the female sex gland from where oestrogen is released and where the ova descend into the fallopian tubes. In birds, only the left ovary is normally functional.

Parasites: organisms which obtain benefit by living on or in an animal.

Pathogens: disease-producing agents.

Perch: a safe place to roost as birds' feet lock when the legs are bent.

Peritoneum: membrane lining the abdominal wall and surrounding abdominal and pelvic **viscera. Peritonitis:** inflammation of the peritoneum, usually serious.

Pin bones: pointed pelvic bones felt either side of the **vent**, three fingers' width apart when laying, one when not.

Pinioning: removal of the **carpus** in wild waterfowl at day-old.

Plumage: feathers covering the body of the bird.

Pneumatised bones: bones which are hollow to reduce weight for flying. They are connected to the respiratory system.

POL: point of lay - usually 18 weeks old. Does not necessarily mean about to lay.

Preen gland: a small blunt protruberance just above the tail, secretions from which help to keep feathers supple when birds preen.

Primaries: the ten main flight feathers.

Probiotics: beneficial bacteria which colonise the gut, leaving little room for pathogens.

Protozoa: often parasitic organisms and include **coccidia**, histomonas, trichomonas.

Pyrethrum: a plant extract (chrysanthemum) used as a safe insecticide.

Radius: smaller and upper of the two middle wing bones.

Ringing: a method of identification. Split plastic rings are put on adult birds and official closed rings are put on young birds.

Saddle: cloth protection for a female turkey from the claws of the male.

Secondaries: the set of wing feathers attached to the **ulna**.

Sex curls: the curled up feathers just above the tail on a drake mallard and domestic drakes.

Sexer: a person who has been trained to be able to sex day-old chicks. Usually only used in large commercial hatcheries.

Sex-linked plumage: where two colours of chickens are crossed and the male and female chicks have specific colours or patterns.

Shank: that part of the lower leg with scales.

Specs: spectacle-like piece of plastic which hooks into a hen's nostrils to prevent immediate forward vision and thus prevents egg eating or feather pecking. Sideways vision is unaffected. Only sometimes effective. Better to sort out the cause of the vice.

Spermatogenesis: the development of mature sperm.

Steroid: basic building block of various hormones.

Stress: the biological reaction (production of cortisol) to adverse stimuli which may lead to disease due to the suppression of immunity by cortisol.

Stressor: any adverse stimulus.

Subcutaneous: beneath the skin.

Tassel: the coarse hair protruding from the breast of a male turkey. Older female turkeys also have a tassel.

Testosterone: male sex hormone.

Thermoregulation: the ability of the body to keep a constant temperature.

Toxin: a poison produced by certain plants, animals and bacteria.

Trachea: windpipe.

Ulna: middle wing bone where the **secondary** flight feathers are attached.

Urates: the avian form of urine which is solid and normally white.

Vaccine: a means of prevention of certain infectious diseases.

Vent: the external **cloaca** of poultry where faeces, **urates** and eggs are expelled separately.

Ventilation: essential replacement of stale air with fresh, no draughts.

Vermin: mice, rats, foxes, magpies, crows, mink.

Viscera: internal organs in the abdomen.

Wattles: fleshy appendages either side of the base of the beak, more strongly developed in male birds. Bright red is an indication of good health.

White blood cells: essential for controlling disease.

Wing clipping: cutting of the **primary** flight feathers on one wing to prevent flight in chickens and waterfowl. Pheasants need the outer three primaries left in place and the rest of the **primaries** and most of the secondaries cut off on both wings. This enables them to glide down from trees or high perches unhurt.

Worms: parasites inhabiting the intestines and **trachea** of birds. These may or may not be seen in droppings and, although normally white, may take on the colour of the faeces.

Zinc: a poison obtained from old **galvanised drinkers** or disintegrating wire netting.

Zoonoses: diseases of animals transmissible to man.

FURTHER READING

Victoria Roberts, *Poultry for Anyone*, 1998, Whittet Books
Katie Thear, *Free Range Poultry*, 1997, Farming Press
Ray Feltwell, *Small Scale Poultry Keeping*, 1976, Faber
Victoria Roberts (Editor), *British Poultry Standards*, 1997, Blackwells
Dr A. Anderson Brown & G.E.S. Robbins, *The New Incubation Book*, 1992,
World Pheasant Association
Victoria Roberts, *Poultry at Home*, video 1993, Farming Press
J.E. Cooper & J.T. Eley, *First Aid and Care of Wild Birds*, 1979, David &
Charles
E. Soothill & P. Whitehead, *Wildfowl of the World*, 1978, Blandford
K.C.R.Howman, *Pheasants, Their Breeding and Management*, (ornamental
pheasants) World Pheasant Association
Dr. D.R.Wise MRCVS, *Pheasant Health and Welfare* (game pheasants), Game
Conservancy
G.E.S. Robbins, *Quail, Their Breeding and Management* (ornamental quail),
World Pheasant Association
Katie Thear, *Keeping Quail*, Broad Leys Publishing (Coturnix quail)
Dr Chris Ashton, *Domestic Geese*, 1999, Crowood
J. Van Hoesen, *Guinea Fowl*, USA
J. Bateman (1989), *Animal Traps and Trapping*. (outof print, but copies are
still readily available.
Dr Clive Carefoot, *Creative Poultry Breeding* , 1988, author

MAGAZINES
Country Garden and Smallholding, Buriton House, Station Road, Newport,
Saffron Walden, Essex CB11 3PL
Smallholder, Newscom plc, Reliance House, Long Street, Dursley, Glos.
GL11 4LS

Fancy Fowl, TP Publications, Barn Acre House, Saxtead Green, Suffolk IP13 9QJ

ORGANISATIONS

The Poultry Club of Great Britain, Sec. Mr Mike Clark, 30 Grosvenor Road, Frampton, Boston, Lincs. PE20 1DB. (Hens, domestic waterfowl)

The British Waterfowl Association, Sec. Mrs Rachel Boer, Oaklands, Blind Lane, Tanworth in Arden, Solihull B94 5HS. (Domestic waterfowl and wild waterfowl)

The World Pheasant Association, Administrator Miss N. Chalmers-Watson, P.O. Box 5, Lower Basildon, Reading, Berks. RG8 9PF. (Ornamental pheasants, partridges and quail)

The Game Conservancy, Fordingbridge, Hampshire. (Game pheasants)

APPENDIX I
MEDICINE CUPBOARD

The following is a list of medicines which I consider essential in my poultry medicine cupboard:

Louse powder based on pyrethrum
Surgical spirit for scaly leg
Tylan 200 injection for mycoplasma
Baytril injection for other infections
Flubenvet wormer to go in the feed
Proleth to go in water against coccidia
Protexin probiotic to go in water, antistress
Homeopathic remedies: Sulphur, Aconite, Arnica
Ivomec cattle pour-on for mites
20g needles and 2.5ml syringes
Scissors for wing clipping
Terramycin soluble powder
Semark pliers

Products mentioned in the text only available from a vet
Tylan 200 injection (tylosin): Elanco
Baytril injection (enrofloxacin): Bayer
Terramycin Soluble (oxytetracycline): Pfizer
Linco-Spectin 100 (lincomycin/spectinomycin): Pharmacia & Upjohn
Emtryl Soluble (dimetridazole): Merial
Vetremox (amoxicillin): Vetrepharm
Ivomec Pour-on for beef cattle (ivermectin): Merial
Proleth (amprolium/ethopabate): special order

Coxi Plus (sulphadimethoxine): Vetrepharm
Apralan Soluble (apramycin): Elanco
Leo Yellow: Leo
Surolan: Janssen

Products mentioned obtainable from agricultural merchants, etc
Coxoid (amprolium): Vetrepharm. Pigeon suppliers
Flubenvet (flubendazole): Janssen. Gamekeeper suppliers or vet.
Protexin (probiotic): Probiotics International. Pigeon suppliers, good
  pet shop.
Johnson's Flea Powder (pyrethrum): good pet shop.
Virkon (MAFF approved disinfectant): Antec International. Pigeon
  suppliers (Vetrepharm) for small quantities, agricultural merchants for
  large quantities.
Antec Longlife 250S (disinfectant for equipment): Antec International.
  Agricultural merchant.
Surgical spirit: any chemist or agricultural merchant.
Semark pliers: gamekeeper suppliers.
Homeopathic remedies: chemist or health shop.
Stockholm Tar: agricultural merchant.
Calcivet (soluble calcium): The Birdcare Company. Bird pet shop.
Nutribal (soluble calcium): Vetark. Bird pet shop
Marek's and other vaccines: Intervet UK, Cambridge

APPENDIX II
SEX REVERSAL IN
AVIAN SPECIES

A project I did for the Hunterian Museum at the Royal College of Surgeons, London (open daily, free entry, a fascinating place)

Sex reversal in birds is not uncommon and almost invariably a female bird changes to a male. This is especially noticeable in sexually dimorphic birds (birds where male and female are visually different) such as the common ring-necked pheasant (*Phasianus colchicus*). John Hunter examined and described such a one, but the whereabouts of the specimen is not now known. In 1982 Professor Roger Short was shown a masculinised pheasant at Perth Zoo, Australia. He suggested the bird be presented to the RCS, and so Perth Zoo generously arranged for the bird to be sent to the UK. It arrived in June 1982, the Australian vet having pronounced it fit to travel but ageing, and it was quarantined at the Animal Care Unit, RCS. Its PCV was 14% and blood smears were watery, NPS, NAD. Oestradiol was 42 pmol/L and testosterone <0.01 nmol/L, both tested by an independent laboratory.

Most laboratories in the early 1980s had much experience of mammals, but little of birds, unlike today. The pheasant was eventually postmortemed in November 1982 as it was elderly, thin and had lost condition. An adenocarcinoma was found on its liver, infiltrating the ovary. The left gonad was oval and had the appearance of a testis with histological findings of seminiferous tubules but no evidence of mature spermatozoa. The lungs had marked postmortem changes and the body cavity was full of fluid. Blood was sent to a medical genetics laboratory but unfortunately chromosomes were not able to be seen. Again, lack of experience with avian specimens proved a stumbling block. The pheasant was mounted in this glass case and interestingly is portrayed as eating an earthworm - a known Hermaphrodite!

Other examples of sex reversal in birds

The Bible warns: 'a whistling woman and a crowing hen are an abomination to God and man' and the ancient Greeks wrote of hens that crowed. Most reports of sex reversal describe other secondary sexual characteristic changes such as plumage. The perennial fascination with 'monsters' over the centuries has produced reports of masculinised female birds, mostly common pheasants. In 1760 Hunter himself wrote 'this animal does not breed and its spurs do not grow ... having all the parts peculiar to the female of that bird.' He went on to describe a further three pheasants he had seen, observing that sex reversal changes occurred 'at an advanced period of an animal's life and (it) does not grow up with it from the beginning ... The following year she had nearly the plumage of the cock, but less brilliant, especially on the head.'

A pied peahen (*Pavo cristatus*) was remarked on, which died in 1775 aged 15, having for the previous three years had a most beautiful male tail. She did grow spurs, but this is not uncommon in normal old peahens. In 1827 William Yarrel stated that 'certain constitutional circumstances producing this change may, and do occur, at any period during the life of the fowl, and that they can be produced by artificial means.' A.S. Parkes in 1940 remarked that 'both Pézard (1918) and Zawadovsky (1922) agree in observing that the castrated pheasant has nuptial male plumage, which Champy (1936) succeeded in feminising with both testosterone acetate and oestrone. From the work of Danforth (1937), who made reciprocal skin grafts between male and female common pheasants, it appears that four different kinds of plumage are produced, corresponding with the four combinations of male and female genetic constitution and male and female hormones. The pheasant thus appears to be intermediate in response between true hen-feathered and normal breeds (of poultry).' Parkes' research at this time was on the domestic fowl.

Poultry with ovarian tumours (incidence 0.0175%) change their plumage to the male type, and can crow, as the ancient Greeks well knew.

There are three breeds of fancy poultry bred especially for their 'henny' feathering: the Sebright bantam, henny Old English Game and Campine. R.C. Punnett in 1937 surmised that there was a special gene for hen-feathering in cocks, but subsequently it was suggested that this was due to a dominant autosomal mutation. If a henny Old English Game cock is castrated it produces male feathering at the next moult. Parkes discovered that 'we have evidence of both a qualitative and a quantitative difference between the response of the feathers of a henny breed and of normal breeds. The normal breed is not feminised by high doses of testosterone, but shows symptoms of the same type of thyroid deficiency as appears in the henny breed at a higher dose-level than is needed for feminisation in that breed.'

Some people have been confused by the eclipse plumage of many breeds of male ducks when moulting; mallard (*Anas platyrhynchos*) drakes in particular (and their similarly coloured domestic derivatives) appear hen-feathered (but are not) as they acquire the same coloration as the females when in the annual moult. Parkes proved that this was not dependent on androgenic stimulation. The Saxony, a domestic duck, was reported in the 1980s as developing male plumage at 3 years old. She lived for another 4 years, retaining her female quack while having the drake's plumage.

More recently, the mandarin duck (*Aix galericulata*) has been reported three times in fifteen years as changing to a paler version of the drake. Only one ovary is normally functional and if this is damaged then secondary sexual characteristics such as male type plumage may occur. A golden pheasant (*Chrysolophus pictus*) in Canada was reported as being a 'transvestite' and silver pheasants (*Lophura nycthemera*) are also known to undergo plumage change from female to male. Black grouse (*Tetrao tetrix*) and ostriches (*Struthio camelus*) join a long list of sex reversal in birds, but it appears to be most common in the Galliformes.

APPENDIX III
CLASSIFICATION OF BREEDS

SOFT FEATHER: heavy

Australorp
Barnevelder
Brahma
Cochin
Croad Langshan
Dorking
Faverolles
Frizzle
Marans
Orpington
Plymouth Rock
Rhode Island Red
Sussex
Wyandotte

SOFT FEATHER: light

Ancona
Appenzeller
Araucana
Rumpless Araucana
Hamburgh
Leghorn
Minorca
Poland
Redcap
Scots Dumpy
Scots Grey

Silkie
Welsummer

HARD FEATHER

Asil (Rare)
Belgian Game (Rare)
Indian Game
Ko-Shamo (Rare)
Malay (Rare)
Modern Game
Nankin-Shamo (Rare)
Old English Game Bantam
Old English Game Carlisle
Old English Game Oxford
Rumpless Game (Rare)
Shamo (Rare)
Tuzo (Rare: True Bantam)
Yamato-Gunkei (Rare)

TRUE BANTAM

Belgian
Booted (Rare)
Dutch
Japanese
Nankin (Rare)
Pekin
Rosecomb
Sebright

Tuzo (Hard Feather: Rare)

RARE

HARD FEATHER:

Asil
Belgian Game
Ko-Shamo Bantam
Malay
Nankin-Shamo Bantam
Rumpless Game
Shamo
Tuzo (True Bantam)
Yamato-Gunkei

SOFT FEATHER: heavy

Autosexing Breeds: Rhodebar
                  Wybar
Crèvecoeur
Dominique
German Langshan
Houdan
Ixworth
Jersey Giant
La Flèche
Modern Langshan
New Hampshire Red
Norfolk Grey
North Holland Blue
Orloff
Transylvanian Naked Neck
Turkeys

SOFT FEATHER: light

Andalusian
Augsberger
Autosexing Breeds: Legbar
                  Welbar
Brakel
Breda
Campine
Fayoumi
Friesian
Italiener
Kraienköppe
Lakenvelder
Marsh Daisy
Old English Pheasant Fowl
Sicilian Buttercup
Spanish
Sulmtaler
Sultan
Sumatra
Vorwerk
Yokohama

TRUE BANTAM

Booted
Nankin
Tuzo (Hard Feather)

APPENDIX IV
GUIDE TO PURE BREED LAYING CAPABILITIES

Breed	Egg colour	Numbers p.a	Maturing	Type
Ancona	white	200	quick	light
Andalusian	white	200	medium	light
Araucana	blue/green	150	quick	light
Australorp	tinted	180	medium	heavy *
Barnevelder	light brown	180	medium	heavy
Brahma	tinted	150	slow	heavy *
Cochin	tinted	100	slow	heavy *
Croad Langshan	brownish	180	medium	heavy *
Dorking	white	190	medium	heavy *
Faverolles	tinted	180	medium	heavy *
Fayoumi	tinted	250	quick	light
Friesian	white	230	quick	light
Frizzle	tinted	175	medium	heavy
Hamburg	white	200	quick	light
Indian Game	tinted	100	medium	heavy
Leghorn	white	240	quick	light
Marans	brown	200	medium	heavy *
Minorca	white	200	medium	light
Old English Game	tinted	200	quick	heavy *
Old E. Pheasant Fowl	white	200	quick	light
Orpington	tinted	190	medium	heavy *
Plymouth Rock	tinted	200	medium	heavy
Poland	white	200	quick	light

Breed	Egg colour	Numbers p.a	Maturing	Type
Derbyshire Redcap	tinted	200	quick	light
Rhode Island Red	tinted/ brown	260	medium	heavy
Scots Dumpy	tinted	180	medium	heavy *
Scots Grey	tinted	200	quick	light
Silkie	tinted	150	quick	light *
Sussex	tinted	260	medium	heavy
Welsummer	brown	200	medium	heavy
Wyandotte	tinted	200	medium	heavy

* most likely to go broody

Some colour varieties of breeds lay better than others, and different exhibition and utility strains exist.

APPENDIX V
MANAGEMENT
& FEEDING

HOUSING

Poultry housing is used by the birds for roosting, laying and shelter. The welfare of the birds is entirely in your hands and certain principles should therefore be observed. The following applies to hens, domestic ducks and geese, guinea fowl and turkeys. Pheasants and quail tend to be kept in aviaries with integral shelter: wild waterfowl are generally too stressed by being housed so are kept in foxproof enclosures with nesting areas.

Space

The floor area should be a minimum of $1ft^2$ ($30cm^2$) for each large fowl or $8in^2$ ($20cm^2$) for bantams. If you can give them more space, then so much the better, bearing in mind they will be spending time in the henhouse sheltering from the rain and wind. Perches should allow a minimum of 9" (23cm) for large fowl and 6" (15cm) for bantams.

Ducks need $2ft^2$ ($60cm^2$) each and turkeys and geese $2\frac{1}{2}ft^2$ ($75cm^2$), waterfowl do not perch except for muscovies who will need 10" (25cm), turkeys needing 18" (45cm). Quail need $6in^2$ floor space and also do not perch.

Ventilation

Correct ventilation is vital to prevent the build-up of bacteria, condensation and ammonia. It should be located near the roof to ensure there are no draughts. It is more difficult to keep the house cool than warm especially in the summer. Waterfowl do better with a drop-down door made of square mesh so that nearly one side of the low hut is open to the air: they tend to sweat up otherwise, which is hardly surprising when you consider what duvets are traditionally filled with.

Window

A window is normally located near the roof with a sliding cover to allow for adjusting the ventilation according to the weather and covered in mesh rather than glass due to the danger of breakage. If more than one window is wanted it is best to site them both on the same side so the house can be positioned with its back to the wind. Egg laying is influenced by the amount of light available - the more natural light the better (for artificial regimes see page 86).

Nestboxes

Should be put in the lowest, darkest part of the house as hens like to lay their eggs in secret places. Size for large fowl is up to 12in^3 (30cm^3) or 8in^3 (20cm^3) for bantams with one nestbox per four hens. Turkeys like 14in^3 (35cm^3) nestboxes. Communal nestboxes with no partitions are useful as sometimes all the hens choose just one nestbox and queue up or all pile in together, which is when eggs get broken. Make sure there is outside access for egg collection. Litter in the nestboxes can be shavings or straw, avoiding hay due to mould, and if the nestboxes have a mesh base, the fleas find it less welcoming. Waterfowl do not need nestboxes, but give them plenty of straw out of which to make a nest. Ducks and geese lay first thing in the morning so, if not let out until 8.30am or later, the eggs will be where you want them. Quail lay anywhere, so do not waste a nestbox on them.

Perches

Even for bantams, perches should be broad: 2" x 2" (5cm x 5cm) with the top edges rounded is ideal. They should be the correct height for the breed so that they can get onto them easily and have room to stand up on them. See above for spacings, but allow 12" (30cm) between perches if more than one is provided. Make sure they are higher than the nestbox otherwise the hens will roost in the nestbox, fouling it and the eggs. If you can provide a droppings board under the perches which can be removed easily for cleaning this will keep the floor of the house cleaner as hens do two thirds of their dropping at night.

You can also check the droppings for colour and consistency more easily.

Security

The house must provide protection from vermin such as foxes, rats and mice. One-inch (2.5cm) mesh over ventilation areas will keep out all but the smallest vermin. You may need to be able to padlock the house against two-legged foxes, and do not forget the pophole which, at about $1ft^2$ ($30cm^2$), will be big enough for most birds, with vertical closing safer than sideways closing.

Turkeys may need a pophole half as big again and ducks and geese prefer a doorway as they seem to have difficulty bending when being put to bed, but if there is food the other side they will go through a tiny space.

Materials

Timber should be substantial for the frame and can then be clad with tongue and groove or shiplap or good quality plyboard. If the timber is pressure treated by tanalising or protimising it will last without rotting.

The roof needs to be sloping to allow rain to run off, but avoid using felt on the roof as this is where the dreaded red mite likes to breed. Onduline is a corrugated bitumen which is light and warm therefore reducing condensation, or use plywood treaded with Cuprinol or Timbercare, which is the least toxic wood preservative to the birds. To protect the plywood roof further, instead of felt use corrugated plastic as it lets the light through and deters the red mite which likes dark places. Square mesh is best on the window and ventilation areas for strength, and sectional construction of the whole unit will make transportation easier. Mesh on exposed wood internally will prevent geese destroying it.

Litter

Wood shavings for livestock is the cleanest and best, straw is cheaper, but check that it is fresh and clean, not mouldy or contaminated with vermin or cat excreta. Do not use hay due to the mould spores which will give the birds breathing problems. Litter is used on the floor, in the nestboxes and on the droppings board. Waterfowl are probably best with straw as they will need more frequent cleaning out than hens.

Floor

The floor can be solid, slatted or mesh. Slats should be 1¼" (3cm) across with 1" (2.5cm) between. If slats are used make sure the house is not off the ground otherwise it will be draughty. Slats or mesh make for easier cleaning out. Waterfowl need a solid floor or fine mesh as they can get their feet trapped in slats. Quail do well on fine mesh <½" (1cm).

Cleaning

Optimal cleaning will depend on the type of litter and the time of year as wet litter needs cleaning more often and deep litter may need the top layer turning over. Weekly cleaning in small houses is probably best, replacing litter in all areas. The best disinfectant which is not toxic to birds is Virkon: this destroys all bacteria and viruses harmful to the poultry and should be sprayed inside a cleaned house once a month.

Buy or make?

If housing is bought from a reputable manufacturer and meets all the basic principles, then that may be the quickest and easiest method of housing your birds. If you wish to make housing yourself, keep to the basic principles and remember not to make it too heavy as you will want to move it either regularly or at some stage. Remember also to make the access as easy as possible for you to get in to clean, catch birds or collect eggs. Occasionally second-hand housing becomes available: beware of diseases, rotten timbers and inability to transport in sections.

Types of housing

There are two basic types: movable and static. Movable pens are good as the birds get fresh ground regularly. Some have wheels which makes moving them easy for anyone. Triangular arks were developed to prevent sheep jumping on housing in the days when different stock was ordinarily kept together, but the shape of an ark can damage the comb of a cockerel. The disadvantage of movable pens or fold units is the limit on size and therefore the number of birds kept in each one. Static or free-range housing needs to be moved regularly in order to keep the ground clean around the house, but the hens are allowed to roam freely or contained within a fenced off area. Tall thin houses are unstable in windy areas so go for something low and broad based. If a sliding or hinged roof is incorporated there is no need to have the house high enough for you to stand up in.

It is useful to have a free-range house with a solid floor raised off the ground for about 8" (20cm). This discourages rats and other vermin from hiding under the house and can make an extra shelter or dusting area for the birds. They are liable to lay under the house if their nestboxes are inadequate. When using movable pens and moving them on a daily basis it is useful to have feeders and drinkers attached to the unit so it all comes with the unit without having to take the equipment out and put it all back again. If you have a stone or brick building to use as a poultry house then this is obviously not movable, so you would get round the problem of disease-encouraging mud at the door by laying slats, mesh, paving slabs or gravel.

When choosing poultry housing go for the basic principles, plus ease of access; if a job is easy to do it is more likely to get done, thereby benefitting both you and your birds.

Free-Range

The EU defines free-range as access to ground mostly covered with vegetation. There is a world of difference between complete freedom of farmyard or fields and a cramped, fenced area in which even fairly inedible

137

weeds such as docks do not have a chance to grow. The muddy patch may be outdoors but is not free range and is definitely a health hazard. If you need to fence birds in, give them ten times as much space as for housing and then double that. With the danger of foxes, some people have a secure run which the birds can be fastened into on occasion during the day or early evening if necessary, but let out otherwise. Flying birds are usually kept in aviaries, planted with shrubs and then sand or gravel on the floor which can be cleaned and raked. Grass can be grown in aviaries if it is seeded and then mesh in a frame placed on top: this allows the birds to eat the grass but not dig out the roots.

FEEDING AND NUTRITION

Use a commercial feed as these have been very well researched and contain the correct balance of nutrients and minerals for chickens and turkeys e.g. chick crumbs, grower pellets, layer pellets or meal, breeder pellets. There are some specialist feeds for wildfowl and pheasants which are well worth using as they are formulated for breeding with more vitamins included. The general ingredients of all feedstuffs are listed on the feed bag label in descending order of weight but few mills will tell you precisely which ingredients they use; they talk in terms of protein percentage, but it is the type of protein which is important. For instance, feathers are protein and are used in some poultry feeds, but this will probably not appear on the label. The finest and best value protein (high bioavailability) as the hen can use it all and therefore needs less of it, is fishmeal. Grain in the form of wheat is a basis for most feeds but more protein and minerals are needed for egg production or breeding. Go for the best feed you can afford in order to produce the best birds. Whole wheat can be used as a scratch feed, that is, thrown onto the ground, but pellets need to be in a weatherproof container: mouldy feed is a direct route to disease.

Meal or mash is not the best as it sticks to the beak and then fouls up the water. Other grains are used when the weather is cold, such as maize, but it is very fattening. Oats have good food value but they are best dehusked. Barley is wasted on chickens as they lack an enzyme to digest it. It is sometimes added to commercial feed with the missing enzyme as barley meal, but waterfowl devour whole barley with relish.

What about additives in feed? There are some antioxidants which give protection for the vitamins for about three months. Always check the 'best by' date on the label, however. Chick crumbs include coccidiostats which is useful as the chicks then acquire natural immunity to the parasite (see page 54). Growth promoters have had bad publicity and some recently have been banned in the EU. These are usually low doses of anitibiotics which are not used for humans and keep pathogenic bacteria at bay in the intestine, thus improving nutritional absorption. The trend is for all antibiotics to be more tightly controlled, so breeders have for some time used probiotics.

These are beneficial lactic acid bacteria and others which colonise the gut and recent research has shown that they have an inhibitory effect on pathological bacteria. Probiotics certainly are effective and have no restrictions as they are feed additives and generally regarded as safe. They are used either in feed or in water and can be fed at any time from day-old onwards. They are useful for combatting stress after a change of environment. The way forward is for these to be included in commercial feed, but it is always useful to have some at hand when, for example, exhibiting.

It is best to use only balanced feeds from reputable sources. Feeding cooked household scraps tends to upset the balanced ration - it is better to let the birds supplement themselves by free ranging on raw greenstuffs, fallen fruit and insects, as they will then eat enough of the commercial feed to provide the correct ratio of minerals, especially calcium and phosphorus. Giving the occasional treat of stale brown bread or fruit will ensure that they come running when you call them, however.

In winter, fresh brassicas and nettles can be hung in the run to provide green food; apples and swedes cut in half, speared on a nail and hung up are popular. Mineralised poultry grit should be available all year round: a large plastic flower pot pegged to the ground with bent wire through the drain holes serves well as a container.

Vitamin supplementation is popular, but not necessarily beneficial as commercial rations are balanced. If there is a specific problem then a specific vitamin may be useful (see page 60). Vitamin preparations are notoriously difficult to compare with each other: their constituents can vary widely, but the best ones are liquid, formulated specifically for birds and added to the water. Some vitamins are toxic in excess such as Vitamin A, so beware of over supplementation.

Herbal supplements can also be dangerous - the ideal is to let the birds find their own herbs in a meadow. Homeopathy is useful and is covered in Chapter 14, page 104.

Feeding regimes - gradually change over several days.
Hens

Chick starter crumbs (20% protein)	day-old to 8 weeks
Chicken grower pellets (18% protein)	8 weeks to 18 weeks
Layer pellets (16% protein)	18 weeks onwards
Breeder ration if you can get it	from 6 weeks before breeding until end of breeding

Some whole wheat from 12 weeks plus mixed poultry grit, maize in winter
Ducks/Geese

Chick (or waterfowl) starter crumbs (20% protein)	day-old to 4 weeks
Chicken (or waterfowl) grower pellets (<18% protein)	4 weeks to 12 weeks
Layer pellets (or waterfowl maintenance) (<16% protein)	12 weeks onwards
Breeder ration, if you can get it, breeding until end of breeding	from 6 weeks before
Some whole wheat or barley plus mixed poultry grit	from 10 weeks

Turkeys

Turkey starter crumbs (24% protein)	day-old to 8 weeks

| Turkey rearer pellets (20% protein) | 8 weeks to 18 weeks |
| Turkey breeder pellets (18% protein) | 18 weeks onwards |

Chicken layer pellets can be used when not breeding
Some whole wheat — from 12 weeks plus mixed poultry grit

Pheasants and guinea fowl

Pheasant starter crumbs (24% protein)	day-old to 8 weeks
Pheasant rearer pellets (20% protein)	8 to 18weeks
Pheasant maintenance or chicken layer pellets	18 weeks onwards
Pheasant breeder pellets (18% protein)	from 6 weeks before breeding until end of breeding
Some whole wheat	from 12 weeks

plus mixed poultry grit

Quail

| Chick starter crumbs (20% protein) | day-old onwards |

Pheasant starter may be better if smaller pieces

If eating eggs or birds, observe withdrawal times for any compounds in the feed. Read the label.

Maize is implicated in several types of mould toxins and makes fat and skin yellow, so feed lightly and in winter for its warming properties.

Water is sometimes called the forgotten nutrient; it cannot be stressed enough that dirty water equals bacterial soup equals disease. Water containers should be refilled with fresh every day and cleaned with a proper poultry disinfectant once a week. If header tanks are used on an automatic system, these must have lids and be cleaned regularly. Winter ice can be as bad as summer shortages due to evaporation. Birds will survive without food for a while, but they go downhill very quickly without water

Summary: give enough space, use commercial feed, avoid mould at all costs (feed or hay/straw), keep water clean.

INDEX

cock 12, 15, 67, 84
colour vision 11, 63
comb 11, 16, 25, 27, 28, 91, 116
commensal 73, 116
commercial feed 138
condensation 133
conjunctivitis 64, 103, 104
copper 100
coracoid 38, 39
cornea 64
corns 26, 28
cortisol 87
coryza, infectious, 99
Coturnix quail 18, 38, 54
cough 67
countercurrent 90, 116
coverts 33, 116
cow hocks 47, 48, 116
cranial, caudal airsacs 66
creosote 102
crop 50, 52
crop impaction 53, 112
crop, pendulous, 53
crop tube 20, 116
crossed beak 28
crowing 67
culling 22, 40, 47, 90, 94, 98, 116

dead-in-shell 60, 106, 116
death 22, 106
deep litter 21
deformities 44, 47, 106
depluming mite 36
Derzsy's disease 97
diarrhoea 54, 55, 59, 89, 97, 98, 100, 105
diet 138
digestive system 49
dimetridazole (Emtryl) 55
disease 7, 10, 20

dished bill 47
disinfectant 20, 54, 116, 141
display 93
Dorking 16, 26, 30, 38
double yolk 83
down 19, 32, 117
downies 18, 44, 45, 59, 117
drench 117
drooping wing 46
dropped tongue 52
droppings 51, 78
drugs 19
ducks 9, 12, 15, 16, 29, 32, 38, 43, 45, 49, 54, 58, 63, 67, 74, 77, 79, 80, 81, 87, 91, 93, 94, 109, 111, 113, 141
duck footed 117
duck viral enteritis 58
duck viral hepatitis 57, 59, 85
duckling 17, 73
dull emitter 86
duodenum 50
dust 21
dusting powder: see louse powder
dustbath 33
dwarfing gene 38, 117

E.coli 58, 71, 85, 103
ear 25, 26, 28, 112
earlobe 24, 25
earthworms 55, 67
eclipse plumage 32, 128
ectoparasites 55
EDS '76 (egg drop syndrome '76) 98
egg bound 83, 112
egg eating 82
egg laying 29, 86
egg peritonitis 83
egg tooth 81
egg washing 57, 82
eggs 7, 9, 15, 25, 35, 55, 60, 78, 82, 85, 105

electric hen 87
ELISA 73, 74, 117
emaciation 89
emphysema 69, 117
Emtryl 55
endocrine system 86
endoparasites 55
endotoxin 117
enrofloxacin (Baytril) 67
enteritis 58, 59, 85, 98, 110, 117
enteroviruses 85
ergots 102
Erysipelas spp. 29, 91
Euphrasia 104
excretory system 51, 61
exhibiting 71
expiration 66, 70
eye 11, 25, 63
eyelids 63

faeces 51, 78
Farmer's lung 69
fast feathering gene 77
fat 14, 61
fatty liver syndrome 61
Faverolles 38
Fayoumi 54, 89, 96
feather follicles 24, 93
feather pecking 33, 60, 87
feathers 11, 16, 31, 33, 34, 44
feed 11, 21, 138, 139, 140
feet 11, 25, 38, 47
female 44, 75, 78
femur 40
flea powder: see louse powder
fleas: see lice
fletching 9
floor 136
Flubenvet 47, 55, 68, 69
fluke 55

flying 90
foam 71
fold unit 117
follicle 24, 93
foot feathers 25
formaldehyde 102
fowl cholera 73
Fowl Pest (Newcastle Disease) 71, 97
fowl typhoid 57, 90, 91
fox 23, 134
foxproof 13, 117
fracture 47
free-range 6, 10, 117, 138
fret marks 34, 118
frostbite 28
fungicide 101
fungus 68, 85
furazolidone 91, 102
fusarium mould 102

gall bladder 50, 51
galvanised drinker 118
game pheasant 122, 123
gamekeeper suppliers 125
gapeworm 55, 67, 70
geese 12, 13, 15, 29, 38, 42, 49, 54, 58, 63, 79, 80, 81, 87, 93, 109, 111, 113, 141
Gelsemium 104
germinal disc 79, 80
gizzard 49, 50, 52, 53
gizzard worm 55
gloves 37
gold 76
golden pheasant 40
goose viral hepatitis 97
gosling 17, 55
gout 47, 61
grain 42, 51, 58, 138, 141

neck 25
neck hackle 25
necrotic enteritis 99
Nene (Hawaiian goose) 26, 95
nephritis 62
nephrosis 62
nerves 93, 95
nervous system 93
nestbox 78, 79, 82, 134
net 15
Newcastle Disease 71
nictitating membrane 63
nitrates 101
northern fowl mite 27, 36
nostril 11, 64
notarium 39
notifiable disease 71, 97, 119
nutrition 32, 42, 59, 138

oats 139
obese 14
observation 10, 11
oesophagus 50
oestrogen 78, 119
Old English Game 12, 24
oocysts 54
operculum 64, 67
oral 20
organophosphates 35, 101
ornamental ducks 81, 117
osteopetrosis 88, 89
ova 119
ovary 33, 51, 77, 78, 80, 119
overcrowding 106, 133
oviduct 52, 71, 77, 78
ovulation 78
oxytetracycline 124

pair 17
pair bond 13

pancreas 50, 52
pant 64
paralysis 94, 95
paramyxovirus 97
parasites 54, 92, 119
parvovirus 97
Pasteurella anatipestifer 73
Pasteurella multocida 73
pathogens 22, 119
peacocks 55, 93
peck 15
pecking order 12
Pekin bantam 14
pellets 42, 58, 140, 141
pelvis 39
penicillin 29
penis 59
perch 28, 42, 47, 119, 133, 134
peritoneum 119
peritonitis 59, 83, 119
perosis 41, 42
phallus 16, 17, 77, 84
pheasants 10, 13, 15, 18, 25, 32, 38, 54, 58, 68, 79, 80, 81, 85, 98, 109, 111, 113, 141
pheasant feed 141
phenol 91, 102
phosphides 101
phosphorus 60, 101, 139
photoperiodic 75
pigment 24, 32
pin bone 14, 39, 79, 119
pineal gland 86
pinioning 13, 38, 44, 93, 119
pipping 81, 82
plumage 16, 32, 119
pneumatised bones 38, 119
pneumovirus 97
poison 53, 62, 91, 100
poisonous plants 100

sexer 78, 120
sexing 16, 32, 34
shadows 63
shaft lice 35
shank 11, 25, 40, 120
sheldgeese, shelducks 59
shell 71, 78, 79, 80, 82
shell gland 77
shell membrane 78
shell-less egg 60, 81, 98
shelter 133
shoulder 25, 39
showpen 15
sickle feathers 25
side hangers 25
signs of health 10, 11
Silicea 104
Silkie 13, 16, 20, 24, 32, 34, 38, 86, 95
silver 76
sinbin 79
single comb 25
sinus 66, 67, 68
sinusitis 64, 67, 68, 73
skeletal system 38
skin 24, 28
slats 136
slipped tendon 42
slug bait 102
small intestine 50, 52
smell, sense of 64
smoke 67
sneezing, snicking 67, 68
snood 18, 24
snow 11
sodium chloride 61, 62, 91, 101
soft shelled egg 81
sour crop 53
space 133
specs 120
sperm 75, 77, 78

sperm storage glands 77, 78
spermatogenesis 86, 120
spine 39
splay leg 40, 42
spleen 52, 87, 98
spur 16, 25, 26, 28, 38, 40, 90
Staphylococcus spp. 28, 85
sternum 39, 65
steroid 61, 120
stifle 40
stomach: see proventriculus
stones 62
straw 68, 134
Streptococcus faecalis 58
stress 15, 20, 60, 68, 73, 83, 84, 87, 96, 98, 110, 120, 139
stressors 7, 58, 120
subcutaneous 20, 120
sulphonamides 74, 102
Sulphur 28, 104
Sultan 38
Sumatra 24, 26, 38
sunlight 22, 61
surgical spirit 37, 109
Sussex 13, 24, 69, 76
swans 58, 65, 67
swimming 63
synsacrum 39, 51, 93
syrinx 67

T cells 87
tail 25, 32, 93
tail coverts 25
tapeworm 55
tarsometatarsus 40
tassel 18, 120
taste, sense of 11, 49
TB, avian 98, 110
tendon 46
Terramycin 124

warfarin 102
water 11, 19, 21, 141
waterfowl 12, 13, 14, 15, 16, 18, 25, 28, 29, 32, 35, 41, 42, 43, 45, 47, 49, 51, 59, 60, 63, 64, 65, 67, 68, 73, 75, 77, 84, 90, 97, 98, 109, 111, 113, 141
wattles 18, 25, 73, 89, 121
webs 26
weight 11, 14
weight loss 105, 112
welfare 10, 93
Welsummer 16, 37, 80
wet feather 35, 36, 112
wheat 42, 138, 140, 141
white blood cells 118, 121
white earlobe 25
wild birds 56, 57, 59, 67, 71, 98
window 134
wing 24, 39, 41
wing bar 25
wing clipping 13, 31, 43, 121

wing coverts 25
wing feathers 31
wing tag 19, 93
wire netting 59
wishbone 39
withdrawal times 55, 105, 141
wood preservative 135
woodshavings 135
wormer 19, 47, 55, 68, 69
worms 47, 55, 108, 121
wound 28
wry tail 47

Yersinia pseudotuberculosis 99
yolk 24, 51, 78, 80, 82, 83, 91
yolk colorant 80, 115

zinc 53, 61, 101, 121
zoonoses 29, 56, 57, 58, 69, 74, 97, 105, 121

Victoria Roberts has also written POULTRY FOR ANYONE, a full colour guide to poultry breeds, which details the characteristics of the breeds, their history and utility.

This book costs £19.99 and may be ordered direct from the publishers: Whittet Books, Hill Farm, Stonham Rd, Cotton, Stowmarket, Suffolk IP14 4RQ by adding £1.50 p & p. Or bought from any good bookseller.